# Rise above the Storms

Clara Moyo

*Overcome Any Obstacle In Life By Waiting Upon The Lord*

authorHOUSE®

*AuthorHouse™ UK Ltd.*
*500 Avebury Boulevard*
*Central Milton Keynes, MK9 2BE*
*www.authorhouse.co.uk*
*Phone: 08001974150*


*All scripture quotations are taken from the King James Version of the Bible.*
*First published by AuthorHouse 11/29/2007*

*ISBN: 978-1-4343-3293-6 (sc)*

*Printed in the United States of America*
*Bloomington, Indiana*

*This book is printed on acid-free paper.*

# Acknowledgements

With special thanks:

To **my husband**, my backbone, for your astounding encouragement, support and patience while I wrote this book.

To **my children** for your fervent prayers.

To our Lord God and to His Apostle and Servant, **Dr Ezekiel Guti and his wife, Dr Eunor Guti,** who He has allowed to accommodate some time in their incredibly busy schedule in the work of God, to contribute to the fruition of this book.

To **Pastor Enock Tigere** and his family, your backing is an explicit testimony.

To **Father Morrow** and all **my brothers, sisters, Pastors, friends.** Without your contributions, this book would not have been complete.

To my precious mum, **Gogo Shongedza,** for your unwavering trust in God.

To my dear late **Dad** and my dear late **Father-in-law,** who were my tutors, educators, for imparting the knowledge and skills I am now using. They fought the good fight, they finished the race. May they rest in peace, safely in the arms of the Lord.

To my beloved mum-in-law **Gogo maNkomo,** for your unfailing love, prayers and being my best friend.

To **Gogo Chibanda,** my Solicitor in Christ, for your support in prayers.

To my mentor and sisters**, Charity Mbewe, Farai Moyo, Jane Maponga,** for keeping my flame burning in the Lord.

To my spiritual parents, **Mr and Mrs Kanojerera**, your days in the upper room were not in vain.

To my editor, **Tapiwa Shongedza,** thanks for allowing God to use your gift of sharp eyes.

To my web designer **Phil Smears** (of sDesign1) and my Administrator **Audrey Mutongi,** your patience is amazing, keep it up.

**May the Almighty God richly bless you all!**

# Foreword

Very often we read factual books based on theory. In this book Clara Moyo discusses Biblical truths intertwined with her personal experiences. Groomed in the Lord by the Gracious Women, Mrs Moyo encountered rough patches while growing in Christ and conquered. Follow on as she shares with you how, through the power of The Holy Spirit, these rough patches amazingly moulded her walk with the Lord. My prayer is that God may minister and strengthen many other souls through this message and that they may be inspired by the knowledge that storms are seasonal, they have got a purpose and are designed for our transformation by the power of our mighty God. Find out why we go through storms when God is there. Stand up to your storms today!

**Dr Eunor Guti**

President of Gracious Women

Ordained Pastor, First Marriage Officer in Zimbabwe

B.A; M.A; D.D. in Ministry from Friends University

The Director of Women's Ministry in ZAOGA Forward in Faith

The Bible says God has a plan for everyone. I know this book was God's plan for mum to reach many people and I know He will make this possible. I pray that God will open up people's inner eyes so that they may see His great power at work in their lives through the Holy Spirit. And yes, the Holy Spirit is at work in this world as I believe this book was not written through mum's own knowledge but under the guidance of the Holy Spirit. Because of this I believe that this book carries an important message for every reader. This message will have a unique impact on each individual and I believe it will yield good fruits. I have seen myself growing spiritually and I have been given inner peace. With God in my life I feel les burdened because I just put all my problems in His hands. He always solves them all.

***Vinnie*** (18 years old)

I thank God for our prayer meetings and home Bible study. These prayers have changed and inspired me in so many ways. Not only did they inspire me, I think they had the same effect on mum when she wrote this book. I feel closer to God and hope this book will help others draw closer to God also.

***Chris*** (13 years old)

I feel blessed and appreciate our prayer meetings. They have helped me know God's love and his power. I have learnt that God knows everything. I believe He knew this book would be written before it was started. I hope that other people will also be blessed by reading it.

*Amy* (9 years old)

# Table of Contents

# Introduction

Isaiah was a prophet inspired by God during a time Israel had been taken into captivity. The Israelites were being punished by God for turning away from Him. The opening chapters of the book of Isaiah explain how they had rejected God's ways and were depending on their own understanding. This consequently led to lives riddled with sin, strife and despair. Then from chapter 40 Isaiah proclaims what God had promised – Comfort and restoration. We will be discussing in particular **Isaiah 40:31-**

> **"But they that wait upon the LORD shall renew their strength; they shall mount up with wings as eagles; they shall run, and not be weary; and they shall walk, and not faint."**

Isaiah talks about faith, dependency and trust in the Living God.

The children of Israel were in exile, the same way we can go in spiritual exile if we are not obedient. But just like the message delivered by Isaiah to Israel, we know we can also look and wait upon God for deliverance and blessings.

We are also in exile here on earth, our home is heaven. While in exile we can experience anguish, disappointments, strife and setbacks, but our Father is always there to hear our prayers and rescue us. He is there to strengthen the weary and frustrated who call on His name.

We live in a world full of hardships, trials and problems which we can not avoid no matter what we do. Prayer after prayer we still seem to fail to get a breakthrough. Life becomes unbearable. We begin to question God's providence and deliverance. This book has the Biblical tools necessary to overcome hurdles. It includes my personal experiences of how I encountered hurdles, trials and tribulations during my walk with the Lord and conquered, moving from darkness to light and from failure to victory through God's mighty power. For years I lacked the knowledge of claiming this power while I had it at my disposal, until the Lord delivered me. I am not saying I am now perfect, far from it, but I had a mighty breakthrough of gaining the knowledge of fighting this spiritual war wearing the full armour of God.

This message is aimed at reassuring fellow believers who find themselves down the valley, stumbling in a storm and thinking they are doomed, those who are hurting and finding it hard to trust God during these painful moments. It illustrates the importance of depending on God's strength and how to endure problems that seem insurmountable through His Word and prayer. The first six chapters are centred on the inevitability of storms in our lives, why they occur, their benefits and how the Lord lifts us out of them if we wait upon Him. The last four chapters take the example of the eagle's characteristics and how we can emulate it in prayer to endure storms.

Storms may seem to be forever and unfair but they only last for a season and have a purpose. We don't pray for problem avoidance but for endurance through God's power as the prophet Isaiah confirmed. By the end of the book I pray that you will have understood the merits of total surrender to God's will in the quest to overcome tribulations.

God is calling us today to surrender all our cares to Him, not to trust in man but in Him. In God we get everlasting solutions to anything bothering us at the moment. We are guaranteed redemption in any form of trouble that man may say is impossible. God answers all our prayers however we ought to realise that the answer maybe a yes, a no or a wait. As such we, at times might not get the exact answer we yearn for. God will always answer in His way, His time and blesses only those that are in His will.

My life was one knotted mess. I grew up going to church but I didn't have a personal relationship with God. Just before my teens I accepted Jesus as my personal Saviour. From then, it took me years to discover how I could live in victory as a child of God. As Christians we have the right to share the blessings of Abraham, to live in victory and conquer what people say can not be conquered. I want to share with you, steps that took me years to lead me, yet in this one message by God's grace, they can also lead you, into a life of victory.

# Chapter 1
# ARE YOU IN A STORM?

***Waiting on God means willingness to do only what God instructs, in His timing, through His power, regardless of circumstances.***

Once we accept Jesus Christ as our personal Saviour we become children of God, entitled to all the blessings promised in the Word of God. We trust God for everything, protection, providence, deliverance and guidance. Then comes a time when we are happily basking in the warmth of God's peace and suddenly we are faced with a raging storm. Typically we go through the normal principles of requesting, praying, fasting, giving, tithing, attending church etc. and do what we think we have to do in the eyes of God, yet we still find ourselves in the storm with the same trials, problems and persecutions. We may struggle financially, physically, spiritually, emotionally, intellectually, socially, academically or occupationally. We may experience failure and disillusion and start to question why God allows these storms in our lives. God seems far and quiet. We stagger and fall in our situation. The burden becomes heavier and more unbearable. Prayer after prayer, there seems to be no answer. It seems to drag longer or even occurring more often. No matter how hard we try we don't find a breakthrough, at least when we think we really need it. So what do we do? Give up and find other channels? Call on to the nearest and most convenient avenue even if it does not glorify God and it is out of His will? The first question we begin to ask is "why Lord?" Giving up and burying our heads in sand seems like the only solution but it isn't.

It is not easy and even impossible to make a constructive decision when you are in turmoil. You may be facing circumstances like losing your job, you can't find one or you are not allowed to work where you are right now. Maybe you do have a job but are facing tribulations there, you have searched high and low for a life partner in vain, your marriage is on the rocks, your children are rebellious, you loose a loved one, a close friend deserts you, you are in financial hardships, or you are emotionally drained and in low spirits. Life's cycle has been perfectly orchestrated like that, you are either in or coming out of one of these storms, and inevitably the process repeats itself.

Storms are an inextricable part and fact of life. We have to grasp right from the beginning that the problem is not the storm, the problem is finding out what God intends to reveal to us by going through the storm. They all come for a purpose. Even if God does not tell us all the intricate details about them, we should be comforted by the awareness that all storms we encounter in life are for a good and valid reason. God does not allow them for fun as He is a God of purpose. We just have to be willing to surrender all to Him. He will see us through the storm and undoubtedly at the end of it we are always blessed and transformed. Bearing in mind that at the end of every season there is a positive transformation should, in itself give us the impetus to persevere. We should not become preoccupied by the storm but allow God to reveal what His plan is for that storm in our life.

I had an interesting experience when I was born again in Christ. I am not sharing my difficulties to alarm you and produce conflict but to help you find peace and comfort within similar circumstances. I thought being born again, accepting Jesus Christ into my heart was a certificate to a trouble free life, but I was wrong. Being born again, as I later learnt, is one important step into being able to bear the burdens with the power of God. I attended church since birth but I only made a personal acceptance of Christ when I was 11. From then on I attended Scripture Union and had a very good Bible guidance from an excellent mentor.

I was obviously not doing what my mentor pointed out in the Bible, because it took me years to learn simple principles. I was probably the most frustrated Christian you have ever known. Most of my friends seemed to find pleasure in things I struggled with, such as fasting all day. By midday I would be looking at my clock hoping by chance it might be six when we should be breaking our fasting. Whenever we prayed they seemed to find inexplicable joy in it, they seemed to have more *appropriate* words to pray with, they spent a longer time than me and their answers seemed to be clearer and earlier. My life was stagnant and uneventful. Simply stated, I grappled.

The suffering continued until God lifted the veil. He showed me that I had to work on acquiring a personal and deeper relationship with Him, not a group prayer only but a one to one talk with Him. I had to painfully learn and accept that every man born of a human being is set for problems while on earth but can be delivered by letting God have His way. I found out that He called me and loved me and most of all that from time to time I would encounter not one, but many problems. The good news I grasped was that God was there to deliver me from all of them, if I allowed Him to. That's when I abandoned my fantasy of a purely smooth sailing, blissful, triumphant and miracle adorned life. Of course happy occasions existed and still do but they have intermittent seasons of difficulties, which only God can solve.

Unfortunately we usually find out what will happen only when it does. The incidents can be different in nature but most of the time the pattern is the same, that is, we go down the valley then up the mountain, and the process replays like that. That is God's law, a law of seasons. God neatly fashioned them differently but we never know what any season bears until we are in it. In each season we sojourn with the promise that God is always with us.

## *A season for everything*

We have no way of choosing which season to be in, neither can we predict which storm we will be facing at any one time, but we can choose how to overcome it by being ready. We can prepare by remaining in the Word of God which never changes. Each season comes and goes and we can not attempt to cling to a favourable one. Seasons come to an end and we enter a new one even if it is going to wipe the smile off our faces. God is our strength-giving and life saving line during the storm and He hears our prayers at the right time (Isaiah 49:8).

In **Ecclesiastes 3:1** we are told, **"To every thing there is a season, and a time to every purpose under the heaven:"** The effects of global warming once caused winter to be too severe and schools had to shut on some days. Summer flowers bloomed earlier and as a result they got damaged by the rain. A lot of many other complications occurred. Flowers should bloom and schools should close but if any event happens too early or too late it causes havoc. The season you find yourself in will pass and if you endure it with a good attitude of waiting on the Lord, you will reap a good harvest. If it is a happy season be blessed and aspire to move from glory to glory and if not pray for endurance. God's timing is perfect timing and His plan is the best, He knows how long your season should last for Him to achieve his Goal in your life. Do not succumb to the temptation of finding a short cut to solve it. You might solve it somehow but without the intervention of God your own solution will be cursed.

We can not outlive any season, unfortunately, nor can we accelerate one so that we can move on to the next one, no matter how appealing it is. Just like our natural seasons, we enjoy summer we plant, reap and we tuck away warm clothes in preparation for winter. No matter how we might fast and pray, winter will always be cold. We can't change it. All we can do is prepare and be ready for it. If autumn doesn't come leaves would not be shaken off and trees are not prepared for winter and it goes on to stop them getting ready for spring and so on.

In our happy seasons we enjoy while it still lasts, preparing and stocking up by memorising verses for the harder and harsher seasons. Not just memorising them, but hiding them in our hearts. During such seasons we take advantage of listening to the Word of God as much as possible, be it on tapes, videos DVDs or from the pulpit. We listen to God as He speaks to us clearly. When we are shaken, we are being prepared for the next season, leaves of old and useless habits are blown off. Without that preparation we will be inadequate to withstand the colder and more severe times.

During hard times, it is too *cold,* we are less flexible, but we should not be depleted, we should have stored up enough spiritual reserves to see us through. We do not stop what we were doing but there are times that slow us down like illness or mourning. That is when we depend on retrieving the stocked up verses and what we learnt before. We can not do without Bible reading or prayer but if the season does not allow it, then we praise the Lord for what He allowed us to store for such times. In difficult times we also depend on our loved ones to pray and intercede for us even more than they did when things were fine. We get time to reflect on ourselves and our conduct with God. The more we reflect the more we grow and get wisdom in Christ through the Holy Spirit.

Life is a mixture of all the seasons and along the way there is a time when the traffic lights will turn red in life's journey and we have to wait. The season of adversities is not forever, although it does indeed seem forever. Life can never be a smooth cruise on the motorway. Even trains and planes have signals. Somewhere somehow along the journey we shall have to wait. It is not a question of *why* but *when*. God works on our lives during these times for a purpose like our natural seasons.

It is up to us children of God, how we embrace them in faith and really take courage in the Lord to benefit something in each one, acting prayerfully not impulsively. We can not avoid season changes, but we can confront them in peace not by might nor by strength but by God's Spirit.

## *Which way?*

The outcome of the seasons is determined by the decisions you take and those decisions in turn will determine your future. The only person who honestly knows the true desires in your heart is yourself. We have to choose one way to pursue in each season. When we make a decision to follow a path, any path will take us somewhere but God wants us to follow one that leads to life. The decision we make right from the beginning of choosing the path, will affect all our endeavours, good or bad. During storms we need to listen to what God is saying about that situation and what decision to make. In storms we will most likely hear a seemingly urgent call from the devil saying time is running out and forcing us to make hasty and unwise decisions. Our Lord Jesus recommends us to follow the narrow way and enter at the strait gate. It should be a decision reinforced by faith or else we will begin doubting along the way. The narrow way is hard and the strait gate constricted but it leads to life. No decision should appear too urgent to circumvent God's insight, plan and command. Wait for his direction and obey it.

Jesus gave us a sermon which teaches us of the best route to take.

> **"Enter ye in at the strait gate: for wide is the gate, and broad is the way, that leadeth to destruction, and many there be which go in thereat: Because strait is the gate, and narrow is the way, which leadeth unto life, and few there be that find it." (Matthew 7:13-14).**

When faced with tragedies and difficulties it is hard to choose the narrow way and strait gate but Jesus is the only Way the Truth and the Life. Few will find it because strait and narrow implies restricted movements, confined to God's Word. The wide road is where most people are treading. Most people live on credit cards and loans, most people get divorced easily, most people do not monitor their children and the list is endless. There are many good reasons why people would have to use cards, take loans, get divorced and so on but the ones the Word of God is against are those who have taken them because they wanted what was easiest, what was more inviting or what they could do effortlessly without consulting God and waiting for His answer.

When we are tossed by storms, the only way to survive is to remain deeply rooted in the Lord. We are required to remain faithful in the narrow way and fearing God to attain victory. The fear of God is not dreading Him or being anxious but it means glorifying, praising and revering Him among other things. The fear of God brings wisdom to help us make the best decision and choice. If we do not seek Him we shall not find. We have to die to self, getting rid of bad tendencies as described in **Colossians 3:5.** We should not entertain any manner that glorifies ourselves not God. This means we ought to forsake the world and seek His Kingdom first, willingly, in fear of Him and in faith.

The season we are going to discuss is the one we encounter while walking the narrow way. It is the dark, cold, windy, icy, down pouring and slippery season. We will discuss a time when you are down the valley, in emotional turmoil, in family crisis, in pain, in defeat, in failure and in despair and how God reveals Himself in such times.

## Why storms?

Trials are weights that build spiritual muscle growth. Storms are often torrential, heavy and severe. They are windy, thunderous and most of the times destructive. Some give a bit of warning, slowly gathering dark clouds, then start pouring but others are more quick and sudden. Whichever type occurs, we can not prevent it, the least we try to do is prepare for it but half the time we realise we were ill prepared. Once they start we have to find shelter and hide. We face them and deal with them until they are over. We find ways to survive them. One of them is to try our best to be ready.

Similarly storms of life are not pleasant. They behave the same way of either striking suddenly like tragedies, illnesses, loss of income and so on. Or they stealthily creep in and then attack like rebellious children who begin with minor misbehaviours to delinquencies, a couple with trivial disputes to a divorce etc. They are destructive but if we hold on fast to the Word of God and believe the Lord is in the storm with us, then whatever was destroyed will be restored. If His goal was to destroy pride He will restore with humility, if it is hate, He will restore with love. In other words any negative element He destroys in the storm will be restored with a positive and everlasting one.

I am reminded of what my sister once said to me. She said that if I do not have a head on collision with the devil it probably means we are driving on the same side. Not that we hope or pray for collisions and storms but their absence is an alarm bell on our spiritual life. Storms are our spiritual barometer and God can allow us to go through them for several reasons. These are only some of them.

### *Storms to demonstrate God's power*

The disciples encountered one on a lake.

> **"And in the fourth watch of the night Jesus went unto them, walking on the sea. And when the disciples saw him walking on the sea, they were troubled, saying, It is a spirit; and they cried out for fear. But straightway Jesus spake unto them, saying, Be of good cheer; it is I; be not afraid. And Peter answered him and said, Lord, if it be thou, bid me come unto thee on the water. And he said, Come. And when Peter was come down out of the ship, he walked on the water, to go to Jesus. But when he saw the wind boisterous, he was afraid; and beginning to sink, he cried, saying, Lord, save me. And immediately Jesus stretched forth his hand, and caught him, and said unto him, O thou of little faith, wherefore didst thou doubt?" (Mt.14:25-31).**

The disciples were in a raging storm already when this happens. It is hard enough to have faith to walk on water when the weather is at its best. The disciples saw Jesus and Peter asks for a command to come out. He asks for the Word of God, the Word which was flesh. Then in faith, he takes three super courageous steps, getting out of the boat, walking in the storm and on water.

Let us recapitulate. We are already in a raging storm of tribulations. It is hard enough to have faith to believe we can do the impossible when life is good. But here we are being required to forsake the social, economic and academic boats we trusted and shift our faith to Jesus. The storm still rages in trials and tribulations. We look in faith within the storm and see Jesus. We want to be sure it is him and we search for a reassuring word to say "come" in prayer. Once we believe we are walking towards Him we should not then focus on any disturbing winds of failure, disappointments and regret that are blowing but on Jesus. Once we take our eyes off him we falter and start sinking into despair. He will be there to lift us up but it is up to us to still reach out again for His hand. We have to stay focused.

This is one of the reasons some storms are allowed into our lives - to demonstrate God's power. There is a time Jesus healed a blind man and confirmed that his blindness was not caused by his parents' sin but to demonstrate God's power (**John 9:1-12**). Jesus revealed to the disciples his mighty power and authority, we too can have that irrefutable hope that He is still the same God who can calm our storms of sorrows. This hope is described in Hebrews 6:12 as our secure anchor for the soul. No matter how fierce the storm is, we have no fear but faith. We can do the supernatural knowing we are firmly anchored in Christ.

### *Storms for disobedience, moving away from God's will*

Storms can be allowed because of our disobedience to His will and His Word. When we disobey God, we drift away from His will. Whatever we are doing then, is nothing but to fulfil our own lusts and illusions. God steps in to make us right with Him and draw us closer to Him.

**"But your iniquities have separated between you and your God, and your sins have hid his face from you, that he will not hear.." (Isaiah 59:2)**. Sin separates us from God. But our God is loving and longsuffering towards us. He sympathises with our shortcomings. He will forgive us if we sincerely repent and ask for forgiveness.

Remember the story of Jonah, who was sent to Nineveh. He disobeyed and ran away and he went to Tarshish instead. **Jonah 1:4** says that the Lord sent a great wind and the ship he was in almost capsized. God calls us back with hostile storms of difficulties to pull us back to His will. I used to plan my things this way. I would have an idea, I would start on it and in the middle of the project I would pray for guidance. God obviously was not interested because when I began I dived in without even consulting Him. I would find myself going back to Him, asking for forgiveness, repenting and starting again.

I had a very costly experience one time. When I finished my secondary education, I decided to go to France where my sister lived.. While in transit, in Germany, I was advised that my visa was not in order and I had to return to Zimbabwe. This was my first time to go abroad and at that time I was excited about taking a flight. That refusal to continue my trip pained me. I asked God why and His simple answer was because I had not listened. It was true I had not just ignored listening to God; I had actually not even consulted him in the excitement. It failed drastically and I had to return home, consult God and I travelled again successfully. I had forsaken the one who is the Way and the trip was disastrous, I found myself in a serious storm.

## *Storms of Omission*

These are storms that occur because of something we omitted, something we should have done and we did not, like forsaking prayer, failing to forgive, to confess our sins or to love, even tithing.

**Malachi 3:8-12** teaches us about tithing. We give back to God what He has given us and when we fail to tithe we are failing to give back what belongs to Him and He calls us robbers. God says we are cursed when we rob Him. A curse is the opposite of a blessing and when we are cursed we are crippled in all sorts of problems. This is when we find ourselves in countless storms as a means of reminding us that this world and its fullness are God's, therefore we should obey His Word.

It goes on to say so that there may be meat in God's house. That means whatever we tithe, ought to be for the glorification of God's house. We are told exactly what will happen when we do tithe, He will pour out His blessings on us and when we do not we are cursed, and when we are cursed we are bound. Our God is a merciful God, who will forgive us when we realise what we are omitting and repent.

Omitting or forsaking prayer is equal to omitting our daily meals. In prayer we communicate with the Father and we can ask Him to reveal to us the benefit or purpose of the storm. We diligently ask Him to expose those areas that we need to address. When we forsake praying, we move out of the light of God into the darkness and we grope. So to get our attention back to Him, God can allow pain to beckon us. He will divert our concentration from whatever is distracting us from seeking Him but one thing He does not do is to force Himself or His blessings on anyone. We can only get clear direction when we abide in Him in prayer. God has no intention of ambushing us therefore He speaks to us in prayer and in the Word.

We need constant prayer otherwise the devil will waylay us in our weakest area and indeed he knows our weakest areas. We should pray that God leads us away from those things we are weak in and try not to associate with them in any way. Pray without ceasing and trust that whatever is revealed can be overcome with the power of God. When the storm is over, you look back and see that your trust in God has developed from strength to strength. You look at what you have conquered like David who killed a lion then a bear and then Goliath the giant.

I resolved to dedicate each day in the hands of God, so that I am covered by the blood of Jesus, my family, friends and my work. The devil can not go near the blood of Jesus and anything covered by it is out of his reach. Each day if I encounter any problems I am assured God will deliver me from them because everyday is a victory when I put it in His hands.

Ask God if the storm has been caused by anything you have omitted that needs attention. Get to grips with it in prayer and His Word for there is no blessing or deliverance when there is a lack of attention to His commands.

## *Storms of immaturity*

Certain tribulations can be allowed when we are not growing. We then get pruned of other unproductive branches in our lives to make us bud. Pruning as the name implies is painful. It demands determination and utter indomitability. Yet if we can only focus on the reproductiveness this pain entails, we will be more than conquerors. Once God prunes us, we get more strength channelled into the neediest areas of our lives. We die to certain attitudes and behaviours and we mature in God's will.

I crossed a rough patch once in this prestigious job I had. I was happy there, I had a good salary and every day I looked forward to going to work. One year I encountered what I thought was an insurmountable problem there. Although I made some mistakes at work, that time I was accused of doing something entirely factually distorted and personally damaging.

I was doing everything I thought I should in Christ. It was one of the most difficult times of my life. I was happy to be surrounded by people who knew God and they encouraged me to press on in prayer. During that time I was amazed to come across certain Bible verses that I did not know. Those that I knew had a new revelation in my circumstances. Eventually God revealed to me that He had better plans for me and I resigned. I was led into a more stable business which led me from glory to glory until I reached a position far much better than where I was.

Only after the ordeal did I realise how strong and mature God had made me. He had pruned my prayer arrangements, my attitude on counselling and I was given strength for more regular fasting. I reckon regular fasting was one of my greatest achievements. God showed me that when I humbled myself with fasting, my prayers were much more powerful. It felt like cutting with a sharpened knife. I chose Friday as my day of fasting every week and to date it has remained a goal to fast at least once a week or more if I am led to do that.

All these reshuffles were brought about by a storm that had woken me up. It made me grow as I was becoming complacent in my comfort zone. I praised God for that pruning period because I recognised the consequences of immaturity in Christ. I took up more duties that I had never thought I would do before, like interceding. I used to think I was busy and doing enough, but at the brink of my job loss, I could not believe how much spare time I had wasted on useless things. I grew.

When my plants, which I planted with passion in the garden, stop growing, I urgently do various things to revive them like spraying, mulching, digging and putting manure. I commit myself to making every necessary change to protect and enhance them. God's dedication to our growth is similar in a mightier dimension. He will work in our lives in different ways, tackling every area that will be impeding our growth. Watch any storm that comes your way and inquire from the Lord if there is any dormant area in your life that requires resuscitation and growth.

## *Faith testing Storms*

Some storms are allowed to test our faith. Abraham went through one such storm.

> **"And it came to pass after these things, that God did tempt Abraham, and said unto him, Abraham: and he said, Behold, here I am. And he said, Take now thy son, thine only son Isaac, whom thou lovest, and get thee into the land of Moriah; and offer him there for a burnt**

> **offering upon one of the mountains which I will tell thee of. And Abraham rose up early in the morning, and saddled his ass, and took two of his young men with him, and Isaac his son, and clave the wood for the burnt offering, and rose up, and went unto the place of which God had told him. Then on the third day Abraham lifted up his eyes, and saw the place afar off. And Abraham said unto his young men, Abide ye here with the ass; and I and the lad will go yonder and worship, and come again to you. And Abraham took the wood of the burnt offering, and laid it upon Isaac his son; and he took the fire in his hand, and a knife; and they went both of them together. And Isaac spake unto Abraham his father, and said, My father: and he said, Here am I, my son. And he said, Behold the fire and the wood: but where is the lamb for a burnt offering? And Abraham said, My son, God will provide himself a lamb for a burnt offering: so they went both of them together" (Genesis 22:1-8)**

Just put yourself for a moment in Abraham's shoes. Would you not shudder to imagine what you might have told the Lord if He had requested such a sacrifice, your only son, one that you might have conceived through heart-rending agony, when you had given up hope, maybe in your old age and at the limit of your waiting? Abraham was called the father of faith. He believed God could provide even though he had not experienced other people receiving God's mercy. We are blessed to have the whole Bible to read about what happened to other people thus fortifying our faith. This happened in Genesis, the first book. The Bible does not tell us what other testimonies had Abraham heard but it tells us that God spoke directly to him. Yet he was still submissive, obedient and trusting in God.

As he left, we are not told whether he told Sara, the son he was going to sacrifice or anyone along the way. When we have important matters God wants to deal with in our lives, I don't think it is wise to go about discussing them with just anyone the Holy Spirit hasn't led us to speak to. I think if Abraham had done that, he would have been under a lot of pressure from different opinions. That would have probably hindered him from executing God's mission. His faith was being tested.

Counsellors are encouraged but consult them through the guidance of the Holy Spirit who will give you discernment. Talking to just anyone is a sign of doubting what God has instructed. It means we need a second opinion and if given in flesh it leads to disaster some people might be jealous and pronounce a curse that will lead to a derailment of God's plan in us. We are told Abraham leaves the following morning. This is astounding obedience. Nothing is recorded about him asking why, regretting or begging God to do the contrary. We hear that he obeyed. He did not hesitate but precipitated, regardless of future consequences.

As stated in the preceding verse it takes three days to get to the mountain. What do you think could have been going through Abraham's mind at that time? Maybe he wished God could change his mind, maybe he wondered why he had to go through the long wait to have a child then be asked to sacrifice him. Whatever did, we see Abraham pressing on, determined and undeterred. Three days is a long wait. But Abraham was a man of faith.

I remember days when I waited for my exam results. Even though I knew I had answered the questions reasonably well, I would be so anxious to the extent that I pleaded with God to make the markers blind to my mistakes. I would pray for good understanding when studying but would start doubting that I would pass. Our God is the provider and we should not doubt that. In which day are you in the storm? Are you just entering, are you in the middle, are you in your third day, seeing the glimpse of the mountain of victory? Whatever stage you find yourself at today, do not give up. Endure it in prayer and God will instruct you and teach you in the way you should go.

Abraham left the men and donkeys at the foot of the mountain. He was going to engage in serious business with God. When we engage in serious matters with God, we go in His presence burden free, in faith and we do not let the right hand know what the left is doing. We present our sacrifice in secret. Isaac asked where the lamb for the sacrifice was and Abraham answered God would provide. That is big faith!

I should emphasise that it is advisable to let everyone know what we are doing and what the Lord has done for us if it is for the glorification of God's name, to encourage and inspire others' faith in God, but once we do it for egoistic reasons it becomes sin. It is vital to check the attitude of our hearts because we reap what we sow.

I am one of those people who used to be very concerned about people's opinions. In fact it put me in bondage for a long time. I became a slave to the numerous people I wanted to please. As such, secrecy was not in my nature. I wanted people to know how much I had given, who I had helped, what I had done. I blew my own horn and it tormented me because it is not easy to please everyone. There was and is only one person I should have cared to please – the Lord God Almighty. The day I found this out, I felt free and I was free indeed. I only had one master to please and he showed me the way by speaking to my heart. I no longer had to make a painful effort to achieve it.

When we are going through these severe faith testing storms, we become stressed and therefore susceptible to obeying any command or any voice that sounds helpful. We are tempted to try any remedy available but God is saying reach out in faith and hold on to my hand, and I will lift you to a safe haven.

### *Storms to prove He is our provider*

> **" And they came to the place which God had told him of; and Abraham built an altar there,**

> **and laid the wood in order, and bound Isaac his son, and laid him on the altar upon the wood. And Abraham stretched forth his hand, and took the knife to slay his son. And the angel of the LORD called unto him out of heaven, and said, Abraham, Abraham: and he said, Here am I. And he said, Lay not thine hand upon the lad, neither do thou any thing unto him: for now I know that thou fearest God, seeing thou hast not withheld thy son, thine only son from me. And Abraham lifted up his eyes, and looked, and behold behind him a ram caught in a thicket by his horns: and Abraham went and took the ram, and offered him up for a burnt offering in the stead of his son. And Abraham called the name of that place Jehovahjireh: as it is said to this day, In the mount of the LORD it shall be seen" (Genesis 22:9-14)**

Abraham tied Isaac and when he was about to knife him the angel spoke to him and a lamb was provided. This was one of Abraham's biggest testimonies. He called God Jehovah Jireh, the provider. God keeps his promises when we wait on Him in obedience. When everything we depend on is gone, God intervenes. This has always been my prayer "Lord, do not let me be ashamed. If this fails, people will not laugh at me, they will laugh at You because I have declared You as my Provider." His Word will not go back to Him without establishing that which He sent it to do.

How many of us believe He will intervene in circumstances that seem perilous, when it looks like time has run out? I know of some incidences when I would trust God but only to a certain extent and when I felt it was the last minute, I would snap and panic. In panic I resolved to all sorts of remedies that were not from Him but my own ingenuity. I would make desperate last minute calls to anyone who listened and to be honest half the time nobody was interested in my petty pleas. I ignorantly evaded the only One who could listen and help me – God. In Panic I failed to wait but the result was that I ended up waiting even longer because my solutions were only temporary.

In **Exodus 20:5** God tells us He is a jealous God. This jealousy is not envy but in the sense of giving glory and honour to someone or something other than Him. Trusting my bank, my family, knowledge, my medical system or anything at all more than God is equal to idolising them and God forbids that. God wants us to put our trust in Him and believe in His providence in all circumstances. As long as we are doing God's will, He will provide. When God says go somewhere, He knows what He has in store for you. He will provide the necessities for the trip and your stay. Elijah in 1 Kings 17 was told to go east and hide. He went east straight away without hesitation. Ravens fed him and God provided water for him from a brook.. This is the kind of implicit obedience God expects from us for Him to bless us and for Him to show His power. When He allows a storm in your life, do not panic, He will be with you through and through.

When I plan a journey, I find out how far it is and how long it will take me. I maintain my car to suit the weather like in winter; I get tyres that are strong enough for snow and slippery roads. I fill the tank in preparation for the trip and if need be I refill it. God knows the intended goal and purpose of your storm, how long it will last and He is faithful to maintain you and give you enough strength to last the storm. He will renew your strength at the appropriate time, the way we might refill our fuel tanks. He allows the storm for a valid reason.

If cars were capable of responding, mine would be at the top of the refusal list because I travel a lot on business on all imaginable roads, dirt roads, muddy roads, slippery, winding ones and all sorts. Its refusal would cancel my journey and my mission would be unfulfilled. This would affect not only me but everyone else I am in business with. That is what happens when we resist enduring a storm. We trivialise God's providence and purpose, His mission in your life ends up unaccomplished. This will not only affect you, but everyone else on the conveyer belt of God's plan.

We gain new revelations and new testimonies when we stand firm in His Word during these tests and lessons. God tests us but He does not tempt us. God tests us to prove certain things such as our trust in His providence. Temptation is from the devil but God allows us to wait on Him and overcome temptation. Abraham's faith was matured. His strength was renewed and he survived the storm. We become more sensitive to the leading of the Holy Spirit. Instead of spending time, money and efforts on things that don't glorify God we are pruned and trained to spend them on those that are pleasing to Him. When we go through any storm trusting God to deliver us, He will adequately provide all the necessities to see us through and we will never be the same again when we come out.

# DAILY WORD OF POWER

And it shall be said in that day, Lo, this is our God; we have waited for him, and he will save us: this is the LORD; we have waited for him, we will be glad and rejoice in his salvation.
Isaiah 25:9

And therefore will the LORD wait, that he may be gracious unto you, and therefore will he be exalted, that he may have mercy upon you: for the LORD is a God of judgment: blessed are all they that wait for him.
Isaiah 30:18

O LORD, be gracious unto us; we have waited for thee: be thou their arm every morning, our salvation also in the time of trouble.

Romans 8:25 But if we hope for that we see not, then do we with patience wait for it.
Isaiah 33:2

Notes:

# Chapter 2
# THOSE THAT WAIT

***God builds character, man builds reputation***

We don't always enjoy waiting. You might find yourself in painful toil and short of what you need while waiting. Waiting purports an inability to control the situation, waiting for something to happen so that you can proceed. You become desperate for an answer and begin to wonder if God is listening. You start asking why you should wait when our God is an Almighty wonder working God who can turn water into wine within seconds, who can do miracles of multiplying a mere two fish and five loaves of bread to feed five thousand people, the God who has counted your hairs and who knew you before you were born, the one who says before you call He has heard and before you ask He has answered? Why the delay?

God's thoughts are not like our thoughts and His ways are not like our ways (**Isaiah 55:8**). For everything He does, He has a good reason, one which, when we patiently wait upon Him, far outweighs what we were actually waiting for.

Maybe you do not want to soar, or you are not facing any problem. Let me advise you that it is extremely prudent to know something about waiting because it is not so much of our choice or a planned agenda to go through storms. No matter what we do we can not escape them, no matter where we are, we are not immune and no matter who we are, they are indiscriminate.

> **"And we know that all things work together for good to them that love God, to them who are the called according to his purpose." (Romans 8:28).**

What a wonderful promise! This is a promise which confirms that in whatever situation we find ourselves in, as long as we remain under the umbrella of the will of God, all things are for our good and He will never leave us stuck in despair for ever. He is faithful to deliver us. He wants us to have victory left right and centre in our lives. Do not be tempted to manipulate the situation or to take a shortcut because all things will work out for your good. Wait.

No matter what your circumstance is, no matter where you are and what you are doing, our God is omnipotent – God all powerful, Omniscient – God all knowing, Omnipresent – God present everywhere, God whose name is I AM, God the Alpha and the Omega- beginning and the end. What man says is impossible, God says it is possible. Nothing is too difficult for Him. He can even extend the delay to teach you to turn your eyes on Him. So we wait upon Him.

## *Active waiting*

Waiting has so many meanings and connotations. Waiting upon the Lord is not a passionless, passive and time killing activity but it is being ready, having hope, patience, in peace and looking for God's intervention in anticipation, with endurance, actively seeking Him.

**Isaiah 40:31** tells us what happens to those that wait upon the Lord when weary:

> **"But they that wait upon the LORD shall renew their strength; they shall mount up with wings as eagles; they shall run, and not be weary; and they shall walk, and not faint."**

Isaiah does not say the richest or the cream of society but those that wait upon the Lord. We will go through how other people have trodden the dark valleys with victory. You will see how pressing on in prayers and leaning only on the Word of God will escort you through the experience of one of God's tools of transformation – waiting. This is waiting while striving to stay in the narrow path.

In this verse Isaiah reveals the key to being able to soar, to run and not be weary, to walk and not faint while in a treacherous season – waiting. You have to wait. Waiting on God is different from positive thinking or ignoring the problems and pretending they are not there. Waiting on God is more powerful, with definite promises and has the Word of God to support you and give you endurance while in pain.

When you wait upon the Lord you do not wait hopelessly to see what happens, but you wait in prayer and in Bible study to seek His guidance. How much endurance you exercise can determine the type of results you wish to get. Your reaction to your problem is also the reflection of your faith. Believe that God's timing is different from yours and His is perfect.

Perhaps you have exhausted all the possible channels and sources of getting a solution and the only option is to wait and see. You are obliged to wait, not by choice but by virtue of circumstances. This is not the kind of waiting Isaiah is talking about. This is blind faith. It is passive waiting. The worst thing you can do is do nothing. Isaiah is talking about waiting like Hannah in 2 Samuel when she could not conceive. She could have tried other ungodly methods to take off her barrenness but she waited upon the Lord year after year. In our time we have medical specialists. Our requirement is to seek God's leading into which specialist we should consult through prayer and God's Word. We have to wait on Him for direction in all our choices and decisions be it specialists, partners, jobs, friends, financial matters and even what we might consider trivial might lead to the answer we were looking for. One hasty unwise step and we could find ourselves in serious problems. God has to be the beginning and the end of our plans. We have to submit every idea and goal into His hands or else the efforts are in vain.

Amidst our difficulties, weaknesses, discouragements, disturbances, depression and inadequacies, when we really feel that there is nothing that can be done, we are given a chance to know how deep God's love is for us and learn to totally depend on Him for an answer by actively waiting. During this period we wait for God's miracles to unfold as we remain in full expectation of His deliverance.

The promises in the Bible are God's pledges for looking out for those who fear and trust Him without doubt. God is calling us to actively and patiently wait on Him until He gives us the solution. Waiting is in no way easy, on the contrary it is agonising because it has no time limit. It runs from seconds to years according to God's divine plan for each of us. Yet time should not deter us from trusting Him. While we actively wait He will be there with us to give us strength, the crutches and the props under our weary arms. All He asks us to do is believe that He can pull us out of the dungeons. If we wait with our hope anchored in God, then our afflictions will be bearable and like Paul, we will begin to count the mighty blessings that the afflictions will bring rather than becoming dejected.

Do not wait passively but actively seek God's guidance and wisdom. Call unto Him and He will answer you. No time spent waiting on the Lord is wasted time. God promised to renew our strength. There are serious repercussions for not waiting. Abraham in Genesis 16-22 thought he had waited too long, he thought he was too old. He was impatient and made a bad decision. God gave Him His grace once more and he was blessed. Do not allow anything or anyone apart from God to influence your decisions on waiting, otherwise you depart from the flock and expose yourself to the wild.

## *Are you in a hurry to wait?*

Our world of technology has become faster and faster. We attend meetings on conference without travelling, we have couriers, we do e-banking, e-shopping, e-mailing, what else is not "e" nowadays when the whole world is at the click of a mouse or telephone button? Thus with this speed, our waiting time span has also been drastically reduced and if we had our own way we would invent e-waiting. Worse still when we wait upon the Lord, time frame is out of the picture. That is a big problem, what then will we put in our most relied upon diaries when faced with uncertainty and our ever trusted planning. Yet His word says **"There are many devices in a man's heart; nevertheless the counsel of the LORD, that shall stand." (Proverbs 19:21).** Many are the plans in a man's heart, but it is the Lord's purpose that prevails.

One time I was deep in financial problems. I had a heap of bills, credit cards were up to the limit and I was deemed not fit for lending. I was so stranded that one day I physically walked into my actual bank and prayed telling God that He is the owner of all the accounts in it. I had fallen into the pit of debts out of foolishness. I had not done my calculations well and I ended up in a total mess. As I came out of the bank I thought I had to do something about it. I met a beggar I know on his way to the shops and I called him and gave him some money.

Still on my foolishness, I withdrew, in fact, overdrew some money for my tithes. I fasted for five days and asked God to forgive me for my foolishness. I quoted Deuteronomy 28:1-14 which details the blessings of obedience. I gave love offerings and that night went straight to God in a sort of challenging prayer telling Him how conscientious I had been in all the episodes. God was quiet. I began to fret and immediately I knew something was wrong. Each time I start worrying I know I am drifting away from God. It dawned on me that I was telling God what to do and when to do it. I was impatient. I repented. That is when He answered. He said He wanted me to know what it was to be in need. I had to be patient. He was going to answer in His own timing and His own way.

God was faithful, three months later He provided a solution. It was not a get-rich-quick one and I doubt He does that. It was going to take me some time to recover from debt. But I was up on my feet again walking on the road to recovery. God is not at all in hurry and we can not push Him to do our things, in our own way, in our own time. When creditors are on your heels, the phone rings off the hook and you fear opening the mail, when the Doctor confirms the worst dreaded news, when going to work becomes a sense of duty rather than a service, when family problems do not rain but pour, when even the people who are supposed to be sympathetic at church and close friends make you feel unwelcome, the last thing you want to do is to wait. You are in constant turmoil.

Waiting in the Lord is the time when you patiently exercise faith and wait upon Him, as difficult as it may be, to wait in anticipation of winning, with the hope for a definite answer and promise. God hears the prayers of those who wait patiently (Psalm 40:1). Those that wait are guaranteed that at the end of the season, they will soar on wings like eagles, run and never grow weary and walk and not be faint, for the Lord promised that His word shall not return to Him without accomplishing that which He sent it to do (Isaiah 55:10-11). If He says wait and you shall fly, then fly you shall as long as you wait upon Him.

You will see what others can not see with an eye like an eagle's. You will glide where others are struggling, with the wings of an eagle. When others are starving, you will eat of the Word, with the strength and determination of an eagle. God will make you endure the pressures of pain and suffering, only if you wait on Him.

## *Be still in God*

Does this sound contradictory, wait actively, not in a hurry and be still? No it is not. I have explained what waiting actively means and the need to avoid short cuts. Be still is referring to being calm and tranquil in the Lord, rendering all your own efforts motionless, making way for God's power to manifest. Be still means save your sweat and seek God's intervention in everything bothering you.

We miss the still and small voice of the Holy Spirit in the din of the world's pressures.

I can not recall the last time I have been still naturally. I am a busy person and I find myself making a tremendous effort to be still. I need to ask God for His grace each time I am in His presence for the ability to be still and embrace His love. **"Be still, and know that I am God;…."(Psalms 46:10)**. That's a sobering thought. Be still and know that you can only depend on Him, that you can not depend on your own strength, that He is the only one you can trust without any doubt, without fear of failure. Knowing Him can never be exhaustive. You can only know that He is God, when you become still, when you cast all your cares on Him, when you totally surrender to His will and wait for everlasting and imperishable blessings. Without total surrender you struggle in vain, get frustrated, ending in exhaustion and finally you quit.

I got married and we had children. From the time I was expecting my first child, I worried about the well being of my pregnancy, when they were born I feared for their safety, health and school. I had little sleep worrying about paying rent and bills. The more I worried the worse it became. Money was never enough. If I got an increment my outgoings followed suit. I was always anxious about something at any one time of my life. I was a Christian with a life in mayhem. My mistake was trying to do things with my own power and might. I was casting all my cares on myself. I was not still. Even when I was tithing, I gave what I deemed enough to suit my budget not *all* the tithe, but any amount I accidentally put aside. That was my biggest mistake.

The Bible, our manual, outlines how we should tithe, give and who we should cast our cares on. **"Casting all your care upon him; for he careth for you." (1 Peter 5:7)**. I was given an illustration of this kind of tithing. I was asked to imagine what would happen if I tried to phone a friend on any telephone number I thought suited me that day or what would happen if I had a prescription from a Doctor and decided to take any amount of medication that suited me and expected to get well.

There was the glaring truth of what I was doing. I was playing games with God, not trusting Him enough to fulfil His promises. Actually I tried to play God. I needed to cast all my cares on Him and let Him solve them.

I needed to be still and get enough time for reflection on God's wonders. If I was serious about leading a fruitful and victorious life the manual was the one I had to follow. Otherwise I was acting like someone using a Sony TV and following instructions from a Philips computer manual. It obviously would not work and if I have any intentions at all of troubleshooting the TV I would have to use the proper manual.

We were created in the image of God and if we try to use any other manual other than the Bible, we are in serious trouble. It is a long process which requires thorough discipline, humility and training. It is not easy to wait while we are anxious and in a state of desperate need but that is the way God trains us to come closer to Him. He teaches us to look to Him and not depend on our own understanding for other alternatives. When He answers, His name is glorified. It is quiet tough to have enough trust on God when there are numerous offers for easy loans, easy dating columns, instant divorce and many easy way out solutions at our disposal. But first ask yourself if they are in the will of God. Waiting on God might be long but it bears permanent blessings.

In Exodus, Moses was still and trusted God in all the tribulations, in 1 Samuel David was still and turned to the Lord for his property to be returned. He could have gone after his enemies immediately, but he was patient, he enquired from the Lord first, and then followed. Elijah in 1 Kings 17 was still, he patiently waited for God's step by step instructions for his nourishment.

It is during these tough times that we come face to face with reality and find out whether we truly rely on God or we faint. There is a promise to those who are still and wait upon the Lord, they will soar on wings like eagles, run and never grow weary and walk and not faint. God promised to meet our needs according to His riches in Christ Jesus, He told us not to fear for He is with us, He invites us to ask Him for wisdom to carry us through our problems.

# DAILY WORD OF VICTORY

I had fainted, unless I had believed to see the goodness of the LORD in the land of the living. Wait on the LORD: be of good courage, and he shall strengthen thine heart: wait, I say, on the LORD.

Psalm 27:13-14

Wait on the LORD, and keep his way, and he shall exalt thee to inherit the land: when the wicked are cut off, thou shalt see it.

Psalm 37:34

I am weary of my crying: my throat is dried: mine eyes fail while I wait for my God.

Psalm 69:3

Notes:

# Chapter 3
# PRAYERFUL WAITING

***We do not pray for trouble free lives, we pray for the ability to endure troubles***

We ought to discuss the value of prayer in our waiting. We will see how in prayer we seek God's guidance, discernment, strength and peace in this chapter, looking closer at the aspect of prayer as our daily bread and our sword to fight the devil. In prayer we speak to our Father and He responds.

Throughout the Bible we see God responding to persistent, fervent and continuous prayers and this should be the same with us. Hezekiah was going to die, but in a fervent prayer he asked God for an extension and God gave him more years (2 Kings 20:1-6). In Genesis Rachel persistently prayed for a child and she bore Joseph and Benjamin. In the book of Ezra people fasted and prayed and God heard their prayers. Jabez in I Chronicles 4:10 made a bold prayer asking God to extend his territory, to be kept from harm and distress, and God granted his request. It is a decision and a choice, not pray and get nothing or to pray and receive. This does not mean all God's answers are a "yes", but they are according to His divine plan as discussed in the next chapter.

I liken prayer to the heart, one of the unseen organs of the body which is so useful that if it stops pumping blood any minute, we are dead. Which other organ could instantly take our lives if it stopped working? Prayer is the invisible warfare we engage in to sustain our lives. Without its function of pumping the blood of Jesus in our churches and our lives, we would not survive.

A story is told of a hunter who had no spear. His friend offered him one on condition that he should come and greet him every morning. He did that for a week while his hunting trips were fruitful. The following week he sent his son and told him to greet the friend on his behalf as he was busy with his day's catch. This happened for several days until the friend realised that his colleague had forgotten where his catch was coming from and he retrieved his spear.

I had a spear retrieval storm that shook me. I used to take prayer for granted. I would not even feel a gap or that nagging feeling that I had failed to do something vital. I would even tell my family to pray for me when they went to church. I would go to bed early and designate someone to say the evening prayers because I was too tired. I often forgot where my day's catch came from until God retrieved the spear. If it was an exam that made me tired and forgot to pray I was certain to fail it. If it was work, then there sure was going to be problems in more than one area at work, the boss, the workmates or even messing up my own work. Jesus Christ our Lord points us to the significance of prayer, He said '..**Simon, Simon, behold, Satan hath desired to have you, that he may sift you as wheat' (Luke 22:31)**. But Jesus reassures Simon by saying that He has prayed for him.

God is our Father and we communicate with Him in prayer. Because we do not fight against flesh and blood, our only weapon in the spiritual warfare is prayer. This one word, "prayer" encompasses a lot of activities for it to be a complete and fervent prayer that yields fruits and results. We must refrain from praying as a sense of duty or praying to appease our minds from the guilt that we have not prayed. We need to form a relationship with our God and humble ourselves before Him, to praise Him, worship Him, adore and love Him in earnest even when we are going through tough times. We come to Him with our petitions, even though He knows everything about us. Bringing our petitions to Him in our own words is an act of surrendering in humility to the giver of all things. We ask Him in prayer, thank Him and also intercede for others regardless of what we are going through. Prayer is not a one way process. We speak to God and we listen to Him with others or in our closet.

When we make our diary for the day is there anywhere we plan some time for prayer? Prayer is sadly usually the side plate extra or a subsidiary of our daily lives yet it ought to be the main schedule. Make prayer your main priority for it is the engine, the think tank, the store room of your soul. Without it nothing will ever function and you will remain stagnant as long as the engine is not started. You will remain motionless with no direction as long as the think tank is not utilised. You will starve to death as long as the store room is empty.

May God make us thirst and hunger for prayer. No matter how hard it seems prayer can never be an option, it's not replaceable. We can't leave it until later one day or later when we have time the same way we can not leave having our meals then decide to have breakfast lunch and dinner at once when we have time.

We have a 24/7 toll free spiritual emergency number **Jeremiah 33:3 "Call unto me, and I will answer thee, and shew thee great and mighty things, which thou knowest not."** Help is only a verse and a prayer away, that number is never busy, you don't need credit to call it. There is no disconnection, Jesus already paid the bill. A dear friend of mine, Fadzai Nkomo, insists that before you call the Pastor, personally call the Pastor's creator first, as **James 5:13** instructs us to do when we are in trouble.

Our times in the closet with God are not for twisting His arm to do what we want. They are special times for reading a short passage with the help of the Holy Spirit, then asking the Holy Spirit to apply this Word in our lives for transformation. We might not see ourselves growing through these daily devotions just as much as we do not perceive instant physical growth in ourselves. It is time to feed on the Word and pray. We then trust God to change us on a daily basis.

We all have different schedules but it is important to fix closet times somewhere before or after a daily chore, that way it is rarely forgotten. When I wake up everyday I head straight to bath. Now, I realised that this is something I can not miss, I might miss breakfast or change my route but I never miss my bathroom trip first thing in the morning no matter what time I get up. So to be sure I do not miss my closet time I have fixed it to be before this trip because I know that the timetable always changes soon after that.

In the next chapter we will look at different prayer principles which yield answers. For now I will expound on some of the ways we speak to God and how we can hear Him since prayer is communication with our Father.

## How God speaks to us

In Chapter 6 I will talk about hearing the voice of the Shepherd and the importance of developing a strong relationship with our Father for us to hear His voice. I believe we all want the assurance that God is speaking and not just speaking but directly to us. How many times have we been advised to seek God's will first and hear what He is saying before we ventured into anything?

I was willing to listen to His voice for direction at all costs but I had no idea how I could hear Him. I had absolutely no clue as to how God spoke to people until He spoke to me through His Word. I enquired from Church ministers and read a lot of Gospel material about this subject and it helped.

I learnt that God speaks to us in different ways. He speaks to every individual in a unique way there fore it is not possible to list every way God speaks to us. Here are some, not all of the ways. One thing for sure is that, when we know God's voice we will not get lost. God is specific when He speaks and has a purpose when He talks to us. He does not give a vague order and leave us to work out what He is trying to say. The moment the message is vague then there is something wrong, either with the condition of our heart or with who we feel is speaking.

God's Word is His will so to know His will we can ask Him to speak to us through the Bible. We have to read it sincerely with the help of the Holy Spirit to guide us for God to speak to us. When I began doing that I would often get a name of a book in the Bible and a chapter imprinted on my heart and till now, when I go through it I come across a verse which stands out or I keep being drawn to. There I find an answer or a message I should act upon. Other people open the Bible and the first chapter they are guided to will contain a message for them. Each of us has a different personal relationship with God and so is the way He speaks to us.

God can speak to us through dreams or visions. When I was a little girl, I would have vivid dreams about something that eventually happened but because I was still young I had no idea it was God speaking to me. As I said, the Word of God cleared the fog. Nowadays if I dream of someone who needs a prayer I take it seriously because I now know God will be commanding me to pray specifically for one of their immediate needs. The Bible records many occasions when people were warned or commanded to do something through dreams and visions. In **1 Samuel 3:8-11** God told Samuel what He wanted to do in Israel while He was sleeping.

Another account is in **1 Kings 3:5 "In Gibeon the LORD appeared to Solomon in a dream by night: and God said, ask what I shall give thee?"** And in Joel there is a declaration that men shall have dreams and visions **"And it shall come to pass afterward, that I will pour out my spirit upon all flesh; and your sons and your daughters shall prophesy, your old men shall dream dreams, your young men shall see visions:" (Joel 2:28)**

God also speaks to us in whispers or by imparting something on our minds. He spoke to Elijah while He was in a cave in a whisper in **1 Kings 19:11-13.** When God whispers we become aware without scepticism that we are being directed to do or not to do something. I have learnt that if I do not obey the whisper, something goes very wrong afterwards. Sometimes it becomes like a burden which will only be lifted the moment I obey that still voice.

God also uses other people around us to speak to us in conversations, through a preacher and even through strangers. When God revealed to me what I was blind to, through other people, I would dismiss it to a mere coincidence only to learn that God does not speak to me in one way.

One day I dreamt of Romans chapter 12. I read it in the morning. I sat down to watch the God Channel while I had my breakfast. The first preacher who appeared was talking about Romans 12 and in particular verse 3. He spoke about faith and emphasised that we should not doubt that we have enough faith to move mountains. That is when I had a mountain of debts. I was struggling financially, I had no savings and that verse was just what I needed. I held on to it, prayed on it, believed it and God's grace met my needs. God's ways of talking to us are limitless. It is us and our unbelief that limit Him. We compare God with our suffering and we make judgements facing the wrong way, facing the problems instead of facing God and we miss His voice.

Whichever way we hear God speaking, it is of utmost importance to ask the Holy Spirit to guide us. Of course, before my strong walk with the Lord I used to tell myself that hearing God speaking only happened to people in the Old Testament and did not apply to me, but I was wrong. We can not denigrate the Old Testament because all scripture is inspired by the Holy Spirit and it still applies today. A closer walk with God will bring us into the fullness of understanding how and when He speaks to us. We will know when it is God speaking because

His sheep know His voice. Not only does He speak to us, He also listens to us when we speak to Him.

## How we speak to God

Prayer is a dialogue with our Father. When we pray, we speak to God, coming into His presence, acknowledging Him as the only Mighty God who is always willing and available to listen and answer. Prayer is as vital to us as the air we breathe, always there and required. Prayer is to our soul as food is to our body. Daily we need to set aside some time for devotions. This is the time we feed the inner man on the Word of God, for comfort, reproof and instruction. During devotions or our closet times, we meditate on God's Word and speak to our Father in prayer.

One of the problems that I had was to know how I was expected to pray a prayer that could guarantee an answer while waiting. I wondered if there was a routine to follow, what I had to say, how long it should be and how I should say it. Maybe you have the same questions. Take heart, I have also been there. I even compared my prayers with other people's prayers. If we were in a group I would listen to what others were saying and lose concentration of my own prayer. Boy, did theirs sound glamorous and more appealing. Mine obviously was not going anywhere. I was ignorant of the fact that God wants us to come to Him as we are, like little children, with our genuine needs not our wishes. I had a hard time speaking to my Father and I always doubted He was listening.

Prayer does not have one formula with set rules. But there are terms which the Bible says we ought to observe for our prayers to be answered like revering Him, asking in His will, making our petitions known, in faith, praying for others, forgiving and so on. We will look into some of them in detail later but the list is not an exhaustive one.

Should the prayer be long or short? Our Lord Jesus Christ warned us, **"But when ye pray, use not vain repetitions, as the heathen do: for they think that they shall be heard for their much speaking." (Matthew 6:7)** A short and meaningful prayer is better than a long and unfruitful one. The strength of a prayer is not within the length but within our focus and the condition of our hearts. If we are not focused our prayers go astray. In Numbers 12 Miriam criticised her brother Moses. God punished her and she had leprosy. In verse 13 Moses made an extremely short prayer in less than 6 words that the Lord may heal her. The Lord answered him. We see the same Moses in Deuteronomy 9:25 making a considerably long prayer. He prayed for forty days and nights for the Israelites when they had made an idol. There are many examples in the Bible of different prayers and it is quiet clear that length is not an issue. I believe their effectiveness is in focus and obedience to what the Holy Spirit is leading you to do. That is why devotions are imperative. They help us know what the Word is saying about all that matters in our lives. We need to focus.

I used to do my daily prayers in haste, while I was absent minded, busy with something like bathing, preparing for work or even driving. I did not have a quiet time of devotions at all. The Lord later taught me that even with my earthly father, I could not discuss important issues in haste. When I have my meals, I take reasonable amounts at regular intervals. My main meal is lunch and I take it seriously. I sit down, relax and eat. When I have a full dinner I begin with starters followed by the main course and then desert. I find it blessing when I enter into such devotions with all stages of warming up, beginning prayer, sinking into deep worship then coming out with a good wash down of thanks giving and honouring our Lord.

Our devotions should also have a designated time in the day and like a main meal requires attentive reverence for that intimate contact with God. It deserves quality time, when our thoughts are gathered together. Of course any time anywhere we can call to God with a short prayer or a whisper but there should be a special time set aside for God in devotion. If I go on for a week on snacks and finger food, my body starts complaining and I am obliged to consider a serious full dinner. Our soul needs similar nourishment and if we are not committed we are risking starving it. Whatever we expect our meals to do to our bodies is exactly what we should expect prayer to do to our souls and to the conditions of our lives.

God looks at your heart to see how deep your desire and will is to speak to Him. **Galatians 6 verse 7** admonishes us not to be fooled because God can not be mocked.

Avoid the insidious assumption that we often make that we can sow flimsily in devotion and reap mighty blessings. The quality of your Bible study and prayer to God *in* your closet corresponds to a true reflection of the quality of your life with Him *out* of your closet. Make an effort, by the power of the Holy Spirit to sow your best in devotions and see how the Lord strengthens and blesses the inner man.

Prayers are done anywhere, anytime because we are encouraged to pray at all times, **"Praying always with *all prayer* and supplication in the Spirit, and watching thereunto with all perseverance and supplication for all saints;" (Ephesians 6:18).** This is why the Bible says **"Pray without ceasing."(1 Thessalonians 5:17)** It means it ought to be regular and we are not restricted by time or positions but the condition of our hearts.

The Bible demonstrates different prayer positions. Consider these:

- standing **"And she said, Oh my lord, as thy soul liveth, my lord, I am the woman that stood by thee here, praying unto the LORD" (I Samuel 1:26)**

- lying down **"And Joshua rent his clothes, and fell to the earth upon his face before the ark of the LORD until the eventide, he and the elders of Israel, and put dust upon their heads." (Joshua 7:6).**

- Kneeling **"And at the evening sacrifice I arose up from my heaviness; and having rent my garment and my mantle, I fell upon my knees, and spread out my hands unto the LORD my God," (Ezra 9:5)** etc.

It is impractical to stand, lie down or kneel ceaselessly to obey the Word of God but I believe the desire in our hearts to keep our minds on the things of God, is a ceaseless voice of prayer. In **Colossians 3:17,23** we are advised, **"And whatsoever ye do in word or deed, do all in the name of the Lord Jesus, giving thanks to God and the Father by him... And whatsoever ye do, do it heartily, as to the Lord, and not unto men;"** Be it work or leisure, what we say and do should be consistent with who we proclaim to be – children of God. We expose our identity by what we do and say. That way, we remain in ceaseless prayer, continuously conforming our minds and hearts to Christ.

Let the Holy Spirit lead your prayer session for He knows your heart and spirit. Ask Him to assist you to bind with the Lord as you wait for triumph in your storm. When you soar up in prayer you will find peace above the storm.

# DAILY WORD OF VICTORY

But thou, when thou prayest, enter into thy closet, and when thou hast shut thy door, pray to thy Father which is in secret; and thy Father which seeth in secret shall reward thee openly.

Matthew 6:6

I will therefore that men pray every where, lifting up holy hands, without wrath and doubting.

1Timothy 2:8

And he spake a parable unto them to this end, that men ought always to pray, and not to faint;

Luke 18:1

# Chapter 4
## PRAYER ANSWERS WHILE WAITING

*God's silence is not His denial*

How many times have you heard an answered prayer being called a coincidence? We have a tendency of saying that because of doubt and a dubious relationship with God. He answers all the prayers. His answer can be a yes, wait or a no, according to His divine decision and will on what is best for us. I could not understand why God could say no but as I grew in Christ I realised that God always knows what is good for me. At times when God said wait I mistook it to mean no. When we ask for the wrong things God says no and when we ask for the right things he can say yes or wait. Just as we cannot trust a toddler with a knife, He says wait until you know how to use what you are asking for. He can not trust me with a million pounds until I know how to use it. He wants you to wait until you seek Him first.

If He always had to say yes, can you imagine what would have happened if He had said yes to Moses when he asked God to end his life in **Numbers 11:15**. He had a lot of plans for Moses to fulfil and He said no. What would have happened to us if God had said yes to Jesus when he prayed that the cup of death pass him by (**Matthew 26:39**)? He would not have gone to the cross to die for us, for our salvation and redemption. Elijah prayed and asked God if he could die. But it was not God's will and God said no (**1 Kings19:4**). Waiting as we have discussed is not easy, neither is accepting God's answer, when it is not what we wanted, but God's will is perfect for us.

The Psalmist said"**My times are in thy hand: deliver me from the hand of mine enemies, and from them that persecute me." (Psalms 31:15)** Our times are indeed in God's hands. Each day we go about planning as if we owned time. When I make my day's programme, I plan it the way I want because I am the one who knows what needs to be done and when. If anyone asked me to do something at three in the afternoon during school term, I would say no or wait because that is the time I pick up my kids from school. In other words, I am the one who would make the best decision about what should be done at any particular time. God also does that when we present our requests to Him. Our times are in His hands therefore He knows when to say yes, wait or no.

Time and self discipline in the Word were a big storm for me. I never seemed to get enough time to set aside for prayer let alone read the Bible. I later realised that there was no way I could have my cake and eat it. Either I was going to forego something and replace it with prayer and Bible reading or accept that my prayers were not going to be answered. I decided to forego a few minutes of sleep in the morning and actually kneel down for a productive prayer as opposed to my superficial prayers I did while lying in bed out of laziness, yawning and buying a few minutes in bed while still struggling to get up. The latter were not sincere prayers and there are no prizes to guess what such prayers yielded.

As I advanced with my walk in the Lord, I have been shown that God will be quiet if, among other things, I pray without the leading of the Holy Spirit, if I pray according to my wishes not my needs or God's will, if I pray in doubt, if what I am requesting is against His will and if I pray holding grudges. I will expand on these later after we have examined the Lord's Prayer as a model of how we should pray as our Lord Jesus taught us.

## The Lord's Prayer: our guide

Our Lord Jesus gave us a good example of how we are expected to pray. He often woke up early and went out later in the day, sometimes all night, secluding himself to be in communion with His Father. The book of Luke, to mention but one of the Gospels, has details of when, where and how often our Lord Jesus prayed. If Jesus, the eternal sinless Son of God, who is God Himself, could not do without prayer how much more do we, people who got the power to be the children of God by grace, need this sustenance day by day. Was Jesus praying because he lacked something? Did He need any material things like we do? Do you see how prayer is an indispensable commitment, not just a requisition, a feeling or a wish? If, when not in want we still have to pray for discernment, guidance, faithfulness and strength as Jesus did, how much more should we pray during storms?

We do not need fancy words to pray, nor is there a stipulated length of time for our prayer to be heard. This had always been my problem when praying. I thought I had to be careful about what to tell God. But as I grew in Christ I began to regard Him as my Father with whom I can be honest. I now tell Him exactly how I feel. I then ask Him to help me get through it.

We do not always know what to say. That is why God sent us a helper, the Holy Spirit. He is always there to assist us when we pray. Even the disciples who were always with Jesus did not know how to pray so they asked him to teach them. The Lord's Prayer from **Matthew 6:9-13,** gives us a guideline of how to pray. In the prayer, I want us to pay particular attention to the order in which the dialogue with our Father unfolds and note how the first three petitions put the Father first before our next three requests. We will examine some of the phrases.

> **".. Our Father which art in heaven, Hallowed be thy name. Thy kingdom come, Thy will be done in earth, as it is in heaven. Give us this day our daily bread. And forgive us our debts,**

**as we forgive our debtors. And lead us not into temptation, but deliver us from evil:.."**

## *Our Father, who art in heaven*

Jesus taught us to address God as Our Father who is in heaven. This means we are very close to Him as His children but still approach Him with that reverence of a Holy and glorious Father in Holy heavenly place. So we begin by acknowledging that God is our Almighty Father. Paul says **"And because ye are sons, God hath sent forth the Spirit of his Son into your hearts, crying, Abba, Father. Wherefore thou art no more a servant, but a son; and if a son, then an heir of God through Christ." (Galatians 4:6-7).** "Abba" was probably not translated deliberately because its meaning is so deep and no English word would convey its meaning with justice. It is a word reserved for the intimate relationship of children and parents. When we call Him Abba or Father, we are confessing that loving relationship we have with Him. David called God the Father of the fatherless (Psalms 68:5) and he also said **"When my father and my mother forsake me, then the LORD will take me up." (Psalm 27:10).**

## *Hallowed be thy name*

Hallowed be thy name means Holy is your name. We do not exalt anyone other than Him. In our prayers we ought to talk more about His name than the devil. When Jesus prayed for Lazarus in John 11 He did not even mention the devil, He began by thanking God.

This is one crucial stage of my prayer I used to totally miss. The name of the Lord to me was just a name but as I grew in the Lord, He taught me that His name was synonymous with what He did. It is not merely a name, it is full of power, glory and authority. He is El-Shaddai- God blesses us, Jehovah-Rophe- He is our healer, Jehovah-Rohi- my Shephed , to name but just a few. Therefore when we say Holy is your name we will be magnifying all the names desiring them to live in us. Psalm 20:1 talks about God's name as a strong tower. In John 17:11 when Jesus was praying for His disciples He asked the Lord to protect them by the power of His name.

We exalt His name, praise Him, honour Him and tell Him how awesome He is in prayer. His name is above all names. Every Father loves to hear praises from their child. Hannah in 1 Samuel 1:11 first calls God ,"Lord Almighty" King David in 2 Sam.7:18-29 said….. "O Sovereign Lord". Exaltation magnifies God, and lack of exaltation magnifies our problems. God knows how mighty He is but He wants us to express our devotion, reverence and honour to Him, yielding to His will. He delights in children who magnify Him in love and awe and give Him the glory and honour which is rightfully due to Him. He then knows we are coming to Him not just for demands but in the full knowledge of who He is.

## *Thy Kingdom Come, thy will be done*

Our Lord Jesus described the Kingdom of God in Parables. In Mathew 13 there are several parables trying to explain to us what the Kingdom of Heaven is like. In all of them we find that the Kingdom is good and we need to make an effort in an endeavour to have it established in our hearts. That is why we need the assistance of the Holy Spirit. He helps us shun all else and yearn for the Kingdom of God to come and let God reign in our hearts.

Once it reigns in our hearts we accept that His will be done. When His Kingdom comes, it removes the sinful desires which dishonour Him from our hearts. We will be accepting to comply with the requirements of that Kingdom we are inviting and "thy will be done" confirms the humble surrender for God to do what He wants the way He wants it done.

## *Give us this day our daily bread*

God designed a spiritual test for believers. He does not give them their needs in one big warehouse. He is the source and we have to go to Him to ask for our daily bread. The daily bread is God's presence in us. We learn dependency on God the Father by asking daily portions of this perpetual supply to our needs. God cares for us and he does not change. In Exodus 16 He fed the children of Israel with daily manna and in 1 Kings 17 we see Elijah waiting for a daily supply of food in drought.

When we say "give us", we are making a request. In prayer we make our requests known to Him. **"…. yet ye have not, because ye ask not."** (James 4:2) Although God knows all the desires of our hearts and what we need, we show humility and exercise our willingness to surrender when we go before His throne and ask.

**"Be careful for nothing; but in every thing by prayer and supplication with thanksgiving let your requests be made known unto God." (Phil. 4:6)** We should not be anxious about anything by offering a prayer of desperation or a prayer of self pity. It should be a prayer with thanksgiving, an indispensable prerequisite, free of anxiety, trusting that, the source of our daily bread will deal with the problem.

From experience this has been what most people including me, considered a prayer, making my requests known. Mine was a prayer with a proper list of all sorts of requests right from the moment I opened my mouth to pray. My definition of prayer was uniquely to ask. Asking is not wrong, it is actually recommended, but we need to know when to ask.

Each time I came home from work, the first thing my children asked before they greeted me was "what have you brought us today?" I had to teach them that it is more acceptable to find out how each one's day had been. If I had brought something then it should always be discussed afterwards. Our Lord Jesus must have had that in mind when he gave us the example of the Lord's Prayer. He does not condemn asking because

He invites us to ask so that it shall be given to us in Matthew 7:7. I am impressed by His timing of when to ask, not at the beginning of prayer because that is when we, acknowledge God, exalt Him, invite Him to minister in our hearts and only then can we ask.

In most cases of our prayer is mainly focused on our own needs but there is a second order that we should pray with thanksgiving. We should rejoice in the Lord always. No matter what the contents of our petition are, we give thanks when we present them to God. Thanksgiving while praying is within the realm of faith. It means we believe our petition has already been answered while we are in petition therefore we are praying a prayer of faith which pleases God.

During prayer we enter into a prayer of adoration, praise and worship. We do not have to follow any certain words to praise God. We can praise in any form, song or talking. One of my Pastors suggested that if I am really at loss on how to praise or worship the Lord I should read the Psalms aloud. They have a collection of songs and prayers of faith, joy, distress and trust in God. They have all kinds of tragedies that I can relate to and their victories. The whole Bible is Holy Spirit anointed so if for some reason you are not led to the psalms open any page for all pages in the Bible are anointed.

### *Forgive us our trespasses as we forgive others*

We have to forgive for, among other things being forgiven also by our Heavenly Father. This means we are also not forgiven if we do not forgive others. In **Matthew 18:23-35** Jesus told a parable about the Kingdom of heaven. He explained how a king forgave a servant. When the servant left he failed to forgive his fellow servant. The king heard about it and he was angry. He got the first servant imprisoned for it. In verse 35 Jesus says that the King did what God will do if we do not forgive others from our heart. When we make our requests we have to confess our sins and ask God to forgive us because our requests can not be granted when we are covered in sin.

Jesus mentions forgiving others. This brings us to another important point of not only thinking about forgiving them but we also have to intercede for them before we conclude our prayer. We are blessed more when we think about others. When we intercede we plead for mercy on behalf of someone else.

This model became part of my daily talk with the Lord. Below I will outline some of the principles, which I took as an attachment to the Lord's Prayer. They opened up a new phase for me and led the grace of God to flow in my life, answering my prayers especially during storms, when life seemed bleak. I believe He can do that for you too.

### *Be Spirit led*

We might not know how to pray but the Bible promises us that we need not worry for the Holy Spirit, our helper, helps us to pray,

> **"Likewise the Spirit also helpeth our infirmities: for we know not what we should pray for as we ought: but the Spirit itself maketh intercession for us with groanings which cannot be uttered. And he that searcheth the hearts knoweth what is the mind of the Spirit, because he maketh intercession for the saints according to the will of God." (Romans 8:26-27)**

To be Spirit led we need to know that the Holy Spirit is our helper and comforter. When we pray in Spirit and in truth, the Spirit will lead us into a prayer that God answers. The preceding verse says that the Spirit intercedes in accordance with God's will. We need to invite the Holy Spirit to fill us daily before we read the Bible and before we pray so that He can help us and intercede for us. The daily filling I am referring to is not baptism. It is in the sense of allowing the Holy Spirit to dominate in us, to posses us and letting Him control us inwardly and outwardly. Sin can make us grieve Him (Ephesians 4:30), He can be quenched (1 Thessalonians 5:19) and He can depart from us (1 Samuel 16:14). That is why we ask for a fresh filling everyday for Him to guide us. This is the time when mighty and amazing things and ideas are revealed to us. Any believer can receive this anointing of the Holy Spirit. When we groan in pain He is there to intercede for us.

The Holy Spirit who helps us pray will also reveal to us who needs our prayer. He will place it on our heart like a burden for us to carry for that person. Usually this burden can go on until the answer comes. We need to listen to Him and follow His leading. When we are led to pray for others during our own storms it does not seem just but I have seen God intervening in mightier ways when He sees that we are capable of forgetting about our problems and thinking about others.

The Holy Spirit is not for Pastors or for certain churches only. It is for everyone who has received Christ.

> **"...... and said unto Peter and to the rest of the apostles, Men and brethren, what shall we do? Then Peter said unto them, Repent, and be baptized every one of you in the name of Jesus Christ for the remission of sins, and ye shall receive the gift of the Holy Ghost. For the promise is unto you, and to your children, and to all that are afar off, even as many as the LORD our God shall call." (Acts 2:37-39).**

Prayer without the leading of the Holy Spirit is arduous. You would need to put a lot of great effort with a questionable result. We need the oil of the Holy Spirit to anoint and lead us in prayer to start with. He has been assigned to help us and He is here already with us. Like I said I was not aware of all these blessings at my disposal until after a closer walk with God. I only had to invite Him like this "Holy Spirit, help me to pray", when I woke up, "Lord fill me afresh with your Holy Spirit" and so the partnership began.

When I get in any sort of dilemma, I ask my helper, the Holy Spirit to help me out, and He is faithful to do it. If we enter into prayer be it for praise, worship request etc. we are entering into a process that needs completion and perfection to attain its intended goal through the Holy Spirit.

Pastor Benny Hinn, in his book *Good Morning Holy Spirit (Thomas Nelson)* shared a powerful message of the Godhead. He said it was like the sun which is one but with three elements, the sun the light and the heat. After I read it the Holy Spirit gave me a corresponding revelation. He said The Father the Son and Holy Spirit are triune. They are like the fire. When we put something on the fire, we are expecting an undoubted form of transformation of the material on fire. The charcoals, flames and the heat are what we call *the fire.* We see the other parts but the heat is not visible. The heat is the manifestation of the fire and it is only existent and effective because we have the fire burning. The heat is the unseen entity which works on the material on or around the fire for transformation. The heat does not exist alone, neither do the flames and together with the charcoals they are *the fire.*

The Trinity is like that. God is like the entire fire, the flames as the Son and the heat as the Holy Spirit. The Holy Spirit is the unseen manifestation of an order from

God through the Son to us. He transforms our requests into the intended goal. The Father commands, the Lord Jesus delivers and the Holy Spirit completes the work. No one goes to the Father except through Jesus. That is why He is called our mediator. The Holy Spirit is the one who transforms our spirit, our souls and our beings according to the will of God through Jesus Christ.

God the Father is the source. When we pray, we pray to God the source with the assistance of our helper, the Holy Spirit through Jesus Christ. We go to the Father through Jesus Christ. As **John 15:26** says:

> **"But when the Comforter is come, whom I will send unto you from the Father, even the Spirit of truth, which proceedeth from the Father, he shall testify of me:"**

The Holy Spirit is from the Father and Jesus will send Him and He will testify of Jesus. They work that way, we ask the Father through Christ, Christ delivers and we receive through the power of the Holy Spirit.

We might not know how electricity operates or see where it is coming from but we acknowledge its existence by its power. We might not understand fully how God works but we can be sure the Holy Spirit is in us by His power, He convicts us. Our hearts beat when we are doing something wrong, we don't struggle to pray, we yearn to be in the presence of God. Our thoughts are renewed and we meditate on God's Word. We aim to speak, do and think about things that are only pleasing to God. We set our standards according to the Bible.

Therefore we ask for the Holy Spirit's leading in prayer to let Him intercede for us because we don't know what we ought to pray for.

Prayer is like a jigsaw puzzle with many pieces that have to be in place for it to be answered. Because we depend on the Holy Spirit to reign during prayer we do not need to crack our heads with what anyone said about the parts of the jigsaw puzzle, we simply follow His leading and each puzzle is different. The pieces mentioned here are not the only ones but merely some from the Bible that helped me hold a prayer in a bigger picture. I believe a sincere prayer in truth and in spirit forms its own jigsaw puzzle and God will answer it.

### *Seek ye first His Kingdom*

Our helper, the Holy Spirit will lead us to the things of God. The Kingdom of God as we saw earlier in our Lord's Prayer has to be established in our hearts. The following verse says we seek it. When we seek something we do some serious searching and it follows that we only seek those things which we are interested in, which are important to us and things we need. Not only do we seek His Kingdom, but we actually have to seek it first, before all other ideas. Are we putting God first in our plans? If not then He is not prepared to bless any of the ones we put first. That is a prescription for an unanswered prayer. Jesus said:

> **"Therefore I say unto you, Take no thought for your life, what ye shall eat, or what ye shall drink; nor yet for your body, what ye shall put**

> **on. Is not the life more than meat, and the body than raiment?........... for your heavenly Father knoweth that ye have need of all these things. But seek ye first the kingdom of God, and his righteousness; and all these things shall be added unto you. Take therefore no thought for the morrow: for the morrow shall take thought for the things of itself. Sufficient unto the day is the evil thereof." (Matthew 6:25-34)**

Not worrying does not mean we should not work. We must work and God blesses the work of our hands. What it means is that we should not divert our attention from God our provider and make it our home work to worry about material things or changing our attention from the giver to the gift. We seek Him first, and *ALL* these things will be added unto us. Yet we find ourselves seeking "all these things first" and secretly hoping God will not notice it or let us off.

Do we not fear losing sight of *all these things* and panic that while we are seeking Him first, then we might miss or lose control of *all these things?* Then we decide that if, and only if we have any spare time, which the modern world rarely has, then we can seek Him. If so our priorities need revision as is a completely wrong turn.

No matter how hard you try to avoid the sequence, God will find a way of stirring you back into course. Evading the sequence only wastes your energy and you end up in frustration because Jesus clearly instructed us on what should come first. This used to be my routine in life and the routine became a mighty storm. I used try to do things my way and using my own knowledge and strength then ask God to intervene when I was half way through the project. The devil really made me busy by giving me the impression that I was doing the right thing, sweating day in day out yet **"It is vain for you to rise up early, to sit up late, to eat the bread of sorrows: for so he giveth his beloved sleep." (Psalms 127:2)**

Most of the things I planned were rarely dedicated to God first or for the purpose of glorifying God. None of these endeavours prospered or gained the slightest recognition. I used to believe I had bad luck. But children of God do not depend on luck because luck is something which comes by chance, something uncertain. Now, the moment we trust in chance, then we are automatically discrediting God's providence and purpose. My lack of knowledge on God's Word made me believe in luck but it was a curse. I was the kind of person who would respond to an advertisement and be told that they had closed entries or stopped receiving applications. If we went shopping I was the first one to be told what I wanted had gone out of stock. If I visited a specialist he would be off replaced by an inexperienced one. I missed buses and trains by seconds. Even if I did the same business in the same conditions as my neighbour, mine did not grow, my debtors never paid me and the list was never ending. I had no breakthrough and I missed chances by inches. Words cannot describe how frustrating, disappointing and exhausting this was. I rate myself as a hard worker, but no hard work came to fruition those days, because I sought *all these things first.*

One day the Holy Spirit led me to a book about a spirit filled woman. I went through it in sincerity. I underwent a time of distillation, purification and refinement. Just visualise the process of cleansing something to remove impurities, extracting coarseness, squeezing unwanted elements. I am not perfect and I doubt that anyone on earth can be, but I can assure you, God did a good job on me and placed me on a different level. He redefined the meaning of a good project to me.

I could see my mistakes sticking out like a soar thumb and I learnt to die to self everyday. That book led me to review my character by Bible standards and I was redeemed. I prayed according to the Word of God and sought His will first. I believed if I changed my response to God, my character and the order of my decisions, then everything around me was going to change too and it happened. Those prayers transformed my entire life. I moved from victory to victory, from glory to glory. It was an uphill task but the power of the Holy Spirit lifted me and I soared like an eagle.

I found out that no one can bluff away seeking things first and then hope to have a prayer answered. It is not possible to sneak in prayers to God, we communicate with Him directly and He sees our hearts and intentions. Seeking Him first is seeking His will and putting Him first in everything and all the promises of "seek, and ye shall find….." (Mathew 7:7), "ask and ye shall receive….." (John:24b) and all the others will fall into place.

I entered into mightier activities that led me to mightier places I had not imagined, not just materially but also spiritually. That verse which says **"Now unto him that is able to do exceeding abundantly above all that we ask or think, according to the power that worketh in us," (Ephesians 3:20)** had a new revelation and it became reality for the first time in my life. It means a lot to me now. It says **"all that we ask or think"**. Believe me the things I ask and think are so vast that imagining God granting them **"abundantly and exceedingly"** is just beyond what my small mind can conceive and comprehend. In suffering, in sorrow, in difficulties or trials, I know there is a living God, waiting to do more than I can expect. He is always there to deliver me from down the valley, up the mountain.

Now each time I miss my step and plan before I tell the Lord, I confess it as sin immediately and repent. This is also one of the many wonderful things our loving God does, He is quick to forgive. Seeking God first paves the way for Him to answer our prayers even when the situation seems very urgent, wait upon Him and seek Him first before you make any move. All the seeking we do is done by faith and we will see how faith and prayer work together.

## *Have Faith*

The Bible is very clear about the inseparability of prayer, the Word and faith. Hebrews 11 tells us what faith is and defines the lives of mighty people of God who had faith in action. I have listed below some of the verses in Hebrews 11 and in brackets I put the interpretation the Lord gave me in relation to faith.

- **Verse 1** (FAITH WORKS IN GOD'S TERMS NOT OUR TERMS )
- **Verse 6** (IT IS NOT ***"hard"*** TO PLEASE GOD WITHOUT FAITH BUT IT IS ***"impossible".*** FAITH DOES NOT NEED EVIDENCE, IT'S UNDERSTOOD IN SPIRIT)
- **Verse7** (FAITH DISCLOSES SOMETHING ABOUT THE FUTURE. FAITH TEACHES THE FEAR OF GOD)
- **Verse 8** (FAITH IS DARING IN TRUST. IT VENTURES INTO THE UNKNOWN FOCUSING ON GOD)
- **Verse 11** (FAITH BELIEVES WITHOUT DOUBT THAT GOD WILL FULFIL WHAT HE PROMISED. FAITH STRENGTHENS AND RESURECTS DEAD SITUATIONS)
- **Verse13-16** (GIFTS PROMISED BY FAITH ARE PERMANENT EVEN WHEN WE LEAVE THIS WORLD. THIS WORLD IS NOT OUR HOME)
- **Verse 17** (FAITH IS OBEDIENT AND TRUSTS GOD'S COMMANDS. FAITH GOES BEYOND HUMAN REASONING)
- **Verse 20-21** (FAITH ANTICIPATES AND FORESEES THE INVISIBLE. FAITH BRINGS EVERLASTING BLESSINGS)

- **Verse 24-27** (FAITH PERCIEVES AND PERSEVERES IN GOD'S WILL. FAITH IS PREPARED TO SUFFER. FAITH IS NOT INTIMIDATED)
- **Verse 29** (FAITH IS NOT DISCOURAGED. EVEN IF THERE IS MIGHTY COURAGE, WITHOUT FAITH IT HOLDS NO WATER)
- **Verse 30** (FAITH IS PATIENT AND NOT DORMANT)
- **Verse 31** (FAITH COUNTS PRIZE NOT COST AND IT HAS NEITHER FIXED NOR PREDICTABLE BOUNDARIES)
- **Verse 33** (FAITH IS AN ASSURANCE WITH POWER AND AUTHORITY TO PERFOM WONDERS)
- **Verse 34-40** (FAITH IS VICTORIOUS EVEN WHEN WEAK, ON OUR EARTHLY MISSION. FAITH SEES BEYOND THE EARTHLY MISSION. IT IS LONG SUFFERING WITH THE HOPE OF ETERNAL LIFE)

The Bible tells us that faith comes by hearing, and hearing by the Word of God. All these mighty people must have heard a Word from God to be so trusting as to wait beyond human reasoning by faith. We need to trust God and after trusting we must act on His Word. If we are only hearers and not doers of the Word then our faith is said to be dead.

Faith is one of the main vital ingredients to an answered prayer. Faith is to prayer as a road is to a car. Prayer and faith are intertwined. It is the pathway on which God's grace is delivered to us. Grace is the unmerited favour we receive from God, not for what we have done or who we are. God is not a respecter of persons (Acts 10:34). We do not even have to try to receive grace because we don't work for it. God gives it to us through the channel of faith. **"For by grace are ye saved through faith; and that not of yourselves: it is the gift of God: Not of works, lest any man should boast." (Ephesians 2:8-9)**

While we are praying we must believe that we have received what we are asking for and God will grant our request. **"Therefore I say unto you, What things soever ye desire, when ye pray, believe that ye receive them, and ye shall have them." (Mark 11:24)** This verse says "when ye pray", meaning even while we are in the process of praying. We are not going to pray then go away and start believing but believe while in prayer. Faith is genuine belief and a deep conviction in God's promises. It needs to grow and this can only happen through prayer and when we read the Bible. Let faith be the way for your prayer to cruise to the throne of God and let it be the way again for God's grace to flow back to you. Watch as faith takes your raw material of petitions, moving them into the processing belt of prayer to the Father and ultimately releasing it back as a finished product of grace.

**Romans 12:3** confirms that we all have a measure of faith that we were given. Even the smallest amount of faith, Jesus said, is enough to move mountains. That measure was given to each of us when we were born again. We live by faith, we are justified by faith, we are saved by faith and faith is the bridge over which God's grace is delivered to us. Even if you have that smallest faith, Jesus said it is sufficient. Wait upon God and pray, ask for His intervention and you will fight the good fight of faith. It is not how big your problem is but how big your God is.

Our faith is only effective when we do what the Word of God says. **"But be ye doers of the word, and not hearers only, deceiving your own selves."(James 1:22)** We should not merely *listen* to the word, and so deceive ourselves but we must *do what it says* if we want our prayers answered. Lifeless faith robs us of the vessel which delivers God's grace to us. When we receive His grace, we receive the answer we have been praying for.

## *Ask according to His will*

God will answer our prayers if what we are praying for is His will, another vital piece. The Bible says in **Hebrews 5:7-8** that Jesus's prayers were answered *because,* He prayed according to God's will *and* He learned to obey because of what He suffered. We seek to establish God's will through prayer and Bible reading because all His promises that are in His Word are His actual will. God knows our minds and our inner thoughts. If what we are praying for is to please ourselves or for self gain then God turns His face away. Therefore before we commit ourselves to anything we must ask for God's guidance and He will lead us to the end.

In our storms we are definitely going to be looking for an answer and a solution. One area to explore in prayer is to see whether we did not get into the storm by forsaking God's will. If that is the case then we need to ask God for forgiveness and repent of it. God is faithful to receive us back. That is why we pray saying "thy will be done on earth as it is in heaven."

In Gethsemane Jesus asked that God's will be done and He was taken to Calvary for crucifixion. Is this not what we define as no pain no gain? Olive oil would not be as good as it is if the olive had not been pressed. Perfume would not smell as good as it does if flowers had not been pressed. Diamonds would not be as precious if they had not gone under pressure. If we are sincere in what we are asking for, we have to be prepared to endure the storms. In them we adapt and grow stronger. Jesus did not remain on the cross, He was buried and He rose again. He went to heaven and received the highest place. If we are in God's plan the grief we go through will only be temporary but necessary for our purification and refining. In due season we come out of the storm shining like germs.

One of my friends Estery Chikerema is an amazing woman of God. I have learnt a lot from her in many ways. She is one of those few people who praise others for their achievements. She admits making mistakes and not only that, but she is willing to address them regardless of what people think. She is honest about how she feels and is not ashamed to share it for transformation. She taught me a principle she calls "bleaching in the Lord". According to her no matter how painful or embarrassing it is in the eyes of the world, as long as it cleanses you to remain in God's will, go for it. I bought one of my sons a car and I was surprised when she called to apologise for forgetting to congratulate me. She said she wanted bleaching in that spot. To some people it is humiliating to go down the line of admitting but Mrs Chikerema is always willing to undergo that painful experience just to remain in the will of God.

Only God's will prevails. In the same breath we need to recognise that obedience is better than sacrifice. If we disobey God, no matter what other good things we do, God will not recognise them. If He says give, we must give, if He says comfort others we must do so. Otherwise He keeps quiet when we send our petitions.

## *Repentance and Forgiveness*

Unconfessed sins hinder the power of God to operate in us. There are times I felt I had repented of everything, but the Holy Spirit would reveal something that needed attention. I repent and confess everyday although I know that the Lord already knows. He wants me to say it myself. At times it is hard to recognise something as sin, but if we turn to our helper the Holy Spirit, He will convict us and we have to act.

Psalms 66:18 says **"If I regard iniquity in my heart, the Lord will not hear me:"** We need to repent almost on a daily basis because usually there isn't a day that passes without us doing, saying, seeing or listening to something sinful. No matter how many times we attend church, as long as our relationship with God is not right because of sin we will not have a breakthrough in our prayers for "............**The effectual fervent prayer of a righteous man availeth much."** **(James 5:16)**. Those that wait upon the Lord, are those that are going to wait with a right mind, willing to confess, repent and to forgive in a way that is pleasing to God.

As long as we harbour grudges and remain with an unforgiving heart God will not respond, as we have already seen in the Lord's prayer. Furthermore the Bible says we should try at all times to live in peace:

> **"Recompense to no man evil for evil. Provide things honest in the sight of all men. If it be possible, as much as lieth in you, live peaceably with all men. Dearly beloved, avenge not yourselves, but rather give place unto wrath: for it is written, Vengeance is mine; I will repay, saith the Lord. Therefore if thine enemy hunger, feed him; if he thirst, give him drink: for in so doing thou shalt heap coals of fire on his head. Be not overcome of evil, but overcome evil with good." (Romans 12:17-21)**

Even if the offender doesn't show remorse or regret, no matter how bad we think the wrong doing is, it is out of bounce to try to revenge. Worse still if we hold on to the grudge and resist forgiving, it is detrimental to self. Failing to forgive brings bitterness and bitterness prohibits God's love to flow in us.

One time I was in a storm. I had a problem with a certain lady I knew but we did not fellowship together. I hurt each time I thought about her. The more I thought about her, the angrier I became. I prayed and asked God to forgive her and myself.

After my prayer I felt good, but later the Holy Spirit revealed that the feeling I had was a selfish one. This was because I had some inner satisfaction of anticipating that God was going to severely deal with her and punish her. I can not rule out the fact that if something had happened to her I would have been happy. It was the opposite of what the Bible teaches us **"Rejoice not when thine enemy falleth, and let not thine heart be glad when he stumbleth: Lest the Lord see it, and it displease him, and he turn away his wrath from him"** (**Proverbs 24:17-18**). It was confirmed by the fact that I could not bring myself to talking to her and I kept thinking about what she had done. It was evident that I had not sincerely forgiven her.

I thought I had forgiven her but when I asked the Holy Spirit to search me, he exposed other areas that I had not honestly dealt with. I read a book on blessings and one of the conditions for blessings to flow was true forgiveness. I had to pray about it again and in the book there was a suggestion of writing down the name of the person I particularly found hard to forgive. I wrote her name down and made it a point that I had to leave the matter in God's hands whether He punished her or forgave her. The way He was going to deal with her, was not my domain at all. I felt liberated after that. My sack cloth was removed and I was girded with joy and gladness. I understood I should never attempt to carry any burdens that are supposed to be in God's hands at any time. We now talk to each other and I don't feel that tinge of hurt anymore.

Let us ask God while we are waiting to search our hearts and see if there is any iniquity in us that might prevent the realisation of grace and prayer answers in our lives. The moment we submit to His call for forgiveness we open closed doors of blessings.

# DAILY WORD OF VICTORY

Rejoicing in hope; patient in tribulation; continuing instant in prayer;

Romans 12:12

And this is the confidence that we have in him, that, if we ask any thing according to his will, he heareth us: And if we know that he hear us, whatsoever we ask, we know that we have the petitions that we desired of him.

1 John 5:14-15

And Jabez was more honourable than his brethren: and his mother called his name Jabez, saying, Because I bare him with sorrow. And Jabez called on the God of Israel, saying, Oh that thou wouldest bless me indeed, and enlarge my coast, and that thine hand might be with me, and that thou wouldest keep me from evil, that it may not grieve me! And God granted him that which he requested.

1 Chronicles 4:9-10

# NOTES:

# Chapter 5
# WAIT ON HIS WORD

*After marking your verses, ask the Holy Spirit to mark your heart*

Our Lord supplied a mighty weapon for us while we are waiting in the storm- His Word, to defy the Herods around us.

> **"All scripture is given by inspiration of God, and is profitable for doctrine, for reproof, for correction, for instruction in righteousness:" (II Timothy 3:16)**

Reading the Word of God was something I found too challenging. It was one of my storms. I dreaded and tried to avoid it when I was young in Christ. At the beginning I felt deterred by the fact that when I read it I did not understand it. At times I had no idea where to read. I gave up reading because I had never actually learnt that I should ask the Holy Spirit to help me with understanding. The only Word I heard was at school, in church services or at meetings. As soon as we finished I forgot what the Word was. In actual fact to me the Word was only part of a confirmation that I was a Christian and I knew nothing further than that. As far as I can remember I do not recall any situation where I depended entirely on the Word of God to conquer a battle during those days. I was completely lost.

Then I had superb Scripture Union sisters Farai, Charity and Jane who I thought, were literally over zealous about the Word. I truly wondered what really their secret was of enjoying something I found so unsavoury. Farai was eloquent and bolder, Charity was the mentor and interpreter of the Word and Jane was loaded with true life testimonies. I was a bit odd, probably not outwardly but inside I was seething at my lack of understanding. One day we went camping in a resort called Kariba. I took a nap in the afternoon. When I woke up I went out of the tent and met Charity. I asked her where she had been. She said she had had hours of Bible reading and prayer. Jane and Farai had done something productive for the Lord and I was *sleeping*. I am ashamed to say it now, but at that time, I was not impressed. I deemed all of them spoilsports. I had the unprincipled idea that when we are away from home or school, we were away from the Lord and we could take a "break" from His presence. That was such a shame but I love the Lord, who loved us before we knew Him. He forgave my old self and led me on to the right path.

As if that was not enough we used to sing:

> **"One thing have I desired of the Lord, that will I seek after; that I may dwell in the house of the Lord all the days of my life, to behold the beauty of the Lord, and to enquire in his temple." (Psalm 27:4)**

I was puzzled why anyone (in fact I branded it as why any normal human being) would want to do that and worse still I thought if they did it, they were probably well faking it.

I rubbed my hands and took a new turn. I resolved to reading the Bible but with a twisted aim. I needed it to join in when there was a Christian conversation and become part of the group. It went on like that for years but now looking back I think during the show off period the Holy Spirit began to work in me. My interest and attitude changed. Bit by bit the Lord opened my eyes and I became aware that the Word and my personal walk with Jesus were conjoined.

I honestly had to repent on my previous trivialisation of God's Word. It was like that incident in **2 Kings 6:17** when Elisha's servant was terrified with the army that confronted them. But Elisha prayed,

> **"And Elisha prayed, and said, Lord, I pray thee, open his eyes, that he may see. And the Lord opened the eyes of the young man; and he saw: and, behold, the mountain was full**

**of horses and chariots of fire round about Elisha."**

That is what happened to me. I was completely blind to spiritual things and depended on my carnal understanding. I had missed the whole point of being born again.

I do not know why I thought I could obey a Father I knew nothing about, let alone what he expected of me. The new revelation was like a gift to me. I began to realise what my friends had when they delighted in the Word of God. Paul said "That I may know Him……" in **Philippians 3:10**. My friends knew Him and He also planted that desire in me to know Him through His Word. It is an indispensable weapon in our spiritual warfare. There is no other weapon more powerful and effective than the Word of God. It defends us, fights for us and protects us.

I will try to fragment what the verse quoted at the beginning of this chapter, **Timothy 3:16** says the Word is for.

## *Useful for doctrine (teaching)*

**"Jesus answered and said unto them, Ye do err, not knowing the scriptures, nor the power of God." (Matthew 22:29)** We will never know anything unless we pay attention to it or learn about it. When we read a scripture, we need to meditate on it and see what lesson we get from it about us, others and God. Being familiar with what we are dealing with gives us the freedom to exercise all our rights.

A story is told of a man who boarded a plane and landed the following day. He met his son and announced that he was extremely hungry. The son asked him if he had not had any meal on the flight. He replied that he did not have any money to buy anything. The son explained to his father that when he purchased the ticket the meals were also included.

We all often make similar mistakes of not being fully informed and end up losing on what is rightfully ours. There is another story of an electrician who charged £1000 for doing a two minute job. On his itemised bill he stated that he had charged £1 for the job but for identifying the fault he had charged £999! Both stories hammer on the importance of knowledge, being acquainted with who and what you are dealing with. I liked a statement from one preacher who said that the only verses that can deliver you in the Bible are the verses you understand. Without knowledge, you can not apply them to your life.

Without reading the Bible we will not know important matters like understanding that when we receive Christ we have been given the right to become the children of God, that He died for us and as a result we are healed, blessed, prosperous, victorious, in fact, all the blessings of Abraham are also ours. We will not know that He paid all the debts we only have to ask for our blessings from the Father. We need to read it in order to learn who God really is, what we should do to please Him, what it is to walk in righteousness, how to live victorious and productive lives. **Hosea 4:6** tells us **"My people are destroyed for lack of knowledge:"** Lack of knowledge is destructive. Without it, you do what you shouldn't or don't do what you ought to and miss God's grace.

When I came to England for the first time, I was struck by the sheer vastness of the motorway network and immediately I told myself I would not drive. The fear of getting lost gripped me and it was worsened by people who said if you get lost on the motorway, you have no way of going back. Because I was not well versed with what goes on and how to get in and out of the motorway, I was trapped in a cage of fear.

One day I drove for training out of town and I met a colleague. I asked him if he had not found it hard to get to the venue and he shook his head and told me that he had used the satellite navigator. I found it interesting and told myself that as soon as I finished the meeting I would go and buy one. I did exactly that and to my amazement, I was caging myself in fear for nothing. There were solutions to set me free. I lacked knowledge and I destroyed not only myself but everyone around me because I would take them the long way when there was a shorter one. I found out that the sat nav was so convenient I could not do without it. It gave me directions, calculated the time, advised me when there was traffic and offered an alternative route. It has so many functions I was not aware of and having it made my life easy.

We have a similar sat nav for our soul called the Bible. It teaches, rebukes, corrects and trains us. The Word of God directs our feet. It tells us where to and what to avoid. It takes us through this life's journey into the everlasting life. That is why David said **"Thy word is a lamp unto my feet, and a light unto my path."** (**Psalm 119:105**) We live in a dark, slippery, treacherous and dangerous world. We can only walk safely in it with the Word of God as our light. Otherwise we would be like those who drive with a satellite navigator that is switched off. It has no use. All we have to do is give it a few minutes a day of study, with the guidance of the Holy Spirit. We can not call ourselves Christians without the teaching of the Bible. Knowledge is power.

The Bibles teaches us that we are in a spiritual war and that the Word is our weapon:

> **"For we wrestle not against flesh and blood, but against principalities, against powers, against the rulers of the darkness of this world, against spiritual wickedness in high places." (Ephesians 6:12)**

As soldiers in this war, we must know our weapon in and out. For my satellite navigator to be effective I had to know where to find the address, the post code, the route, the map, how to avoid a certain road etc. It is the same with the Word of God as our weapon we need to know what it teaches about healing, prosperity, joy, victory and all the spiritual blessings God promised us. Once we know all these promises, then we can proclaim them and apply them to our lives. Even in the darkest hour, we have many promises of redemption from God. As long as we are willing to pray for revelation, God is faithful to grant it.

## *Reproof (Rebuking)*

Paul says the Word of God rebukes. It rebukes sin and gives us the expected standards of a Christ like nature. I have a problem with friends who tell me "not to worry about the mess" when I visit them. Or those who say that they have a *weakness* with temper. I am worried about the mess because the home is supposed to be a safe haven, clean and welcoming, where angels guard us when we sleep. A one day mess is excusable but not a permanent occurrence. Temper is not just a *weakness,* it is a huge problem. The Bible points it out and tells us to deal with such problems effectively not just name and list them. We ought to rebuke that untidiness and those hot tempers.

The Word of God can work in us by the power of the Holy Spirit which transforms us. It rebukes the sinful natures in our lives. There was a time when I would talk about debts as if they were prestigious. While it is not sinful to borrow for necessities like buying a house or study, my borrowing had turned into sin and a storm because it began controlling me. It emanated more from greed, impatience and ignorance of managing finances. It ended up being a burden and I think I even caused non believers to doubt the power of God's provision through my lacking, yet it had been caused by my own foolishness. At times I failed to meet my loan repayments, contrary to what the Bible says **"Owe no man any thing, but to love one another: for he that loveth another hath fulfilled the law." (Romans 13:8)**

The Bible tells us:

> **"For the Lord thy God blesseth thee, as he promised thee: and thou shalt lend unto many nations, but thou shalt not borrow; and thou shalt reign over many nations, but they shall not reign over thee." (Deutoronomy 15:6) and "The Lord shall open unto thee his good treasure, the heaven to give the rain unto thy land in his season, and to bless all the work of thine hand: and thou shalt lend unto many nations, and thou shalt not borrow." (Deuteronomy 28:12)**

Even after reading this, I did not make any efforts to pray that God allows me to get out of debt. I struggled a lot and all along, the Word was there to help me rebuke lacking and proclaim this prosperity that God promised. I thank God He eventually revealed the solution to me.

The debts did not disappear immediately as if a magic wand had been waved but with the power of the Holy Spirit I solved other underlying root problems while dealing with debts. I had to cut off the roots that led me into debt. I had to discipline myself to wait until I could afford to buy something. My husband helped me to put credit cards away. He also advised me if ever we needed to use them we should agree to discuss it first. The Bible rebuked the spirit of eating my seed. No matter how low my income was, I still had to tithe and give. Many things changed in me.

**Hebrews 4:12** says,

> **"For the word of God is quick, and powerful, and sharper than any twoedged sword, piercing even to the dividing asunder of soul and spirit, and of the joints and marrow, and is a discerner of the thoughts and intents of the heart."**

This is our weapon to fight the devil when he brings doubt and fear, when he brings lies and intimidation. The Word of God rebukes. When the devil attacks us, we rebuke him by the Word of God, we will not accept what he presents in our lives, but we will tell him what is written and he will flee.

We are commanded to meditate on this Word day and night (Joshua 1:8). When Jesus was tempted He told the devil what was written in the Word of God. That is the only tool the devil fears because the Word is God. When we pray with the Word, we are claiming the promises that God made for us – healing, deliverance, blessings, victory etc.

A sword in its sheath is useless. The Word has to be read, spoken and obeyed for it to work. It will rebuke any manner of sin that tempts us and as long as we keep it as our weapon, we will win the battle. We have to be sure when to attack and who we are attacking. We remain assured that God will do what He said He would because He keeps His promises. We are working with a weapon that is *living* and *active*. This means that as we are in the battle it will transform the situation and ourselves too. While it judges our thoughts and attitudes, it rebukes the undesirable and cleanses us.

In High school we had a school badge that had 3 legs connected in the middle to look like a wheel. It had a motto written in Latin which translated to "Whichever way you turn me, I will stand". Some years later I was asked to give the Word at a prayer meeting. As I was praying for the Word I was given Hebrews 4:12. The badge was brought into my mind and I had a revelation that the Word which is sharper than any double edged sword could do what those legs did, whichever way I swung it, it could cut. In the midst of illness it cuts, poverty, it cuts, defeat, it cuts, depression it cuts, you name it, and it cuts. In the Old Testament we see God, striking wrong doers. In the New Testament Jesus rebukes and the Spirit convicts. Jesus is the Word that became flesh and lived among us. He rebuked and He still does.

## *Correcting*

David said **"Thy word have I hid in mine heart, that I might not sin against thee." (Psalms 119:11)** If the Word is not buried in our hearts, we do as we please because we have no measuring stick or standard to guide us. At school we likened it to a mirror which shows you what needs to be corrected. When you look in a mirror you see exactly your own image not someone else's, with all the details as they are. When we read the Bible we look into a spiritual mirror which reflects what we are and points out what we need to put straight with the Lord. We do not just look in the mirror, realise there is a mistake and go away. We fix the problem while we are still looking to see that it has been dealt with.

Even when we are convinced that there is nothing wrong, we often dash to the mirror as final assurance before going out. I mentioned before that when I was young, I had really vivid dreams. I began looking forward to going to bed to dream. This is the sort of passion God has now led me to about reading the Bible for correction. I look forward to reading it to find out what God wants to tell me. I now have a small pocket size one that I keep in my bag to read any time.

**"Is not my word like as a fire? saith the Lord; and like a hammer that breaketh the rock in pieces?" (Jeremiah 23:29)** When we are in the Word of God, He melts our bad habits and moulds us to what He desires us to be. He shatters the works of the devil and seals us with the blood of Jesus. A certain purifier explained how purifiers of metal let the metal melt on the fire while they are watching it and they know it is done when they see their image in the melted metal. God is watching us while He purifies us. He knows we are complete when He sees His image in us. God is a loving God. When we decide to follow Him, we make a serious commitment. This kind of commitment means denying self to the extent of allowing His hammer to shatter the undesirables in us with the power of the Holy Spirit, through Our Lord Jesus and become like Christ.

Correction is not easy to go through because in the first place you might not think or know there is something wrong or what actually is wrong. When you do, you could go into denial. This is why we have to ask God to search us, to depend on the Word to direct us and be willing to be corrected. May the Lord give us the desire to read the Word for correction.

## *Instruction (Training)*

I can not remember anything that I have done well without practicing. I think it applies to most of us, without training there is no miracle of success. When I got married I joined the Gracious Women group. We had a hard working mighty woman of God as the leader called Mrs Chikono. Mrs Chikono was and still is a mother in Christ to many. One particular thing she taught me that sank in my heart up to now was that marriage is the only institution where you receive the Certificate before the training. She therefore emphasised to me how much I had to read the Word for training in the union I had entered with my husband. Like most marriages, we encountered storms and very rough patches but each time we sought advice from Mrs Chikono, she always quoted from the Word of God and rightly put her hands up saying it was not from her, but that is what the Lord was saying. Some of the advice was hard to accept, especially when I thought I was right but no beneficial training is ever without pain.

Gracious Women's weapon, the Word of God, groomed me. I was taught, among other things, to have a sweet spirit, to be quick listen but slow to talk, to personally take the responsibility of teaching my children the Word, otherwise someone else was going to do it in their own way. They trained us with the Word and it proves everlasting.

I will not cease praising and do not think I shall thank the Lord enough for His power that I drew from the instruction of His Word to endure the storms. I now have children and we have the usual storms of raising them. I still call Mrs Chikono and she still gives me verses to overcome adversities.

Paul in **1 Corinthians 9:24-27** spoke about our Christian life in terms of a race,

> **"Know ye not that they which run in a race run all, but one receiveth the prize? So run, that ye may obtain. And every man that striveth for the mastery is temperate in all things. Now they do it to obtain a corruptible crown; but we an incorruptible. I therefore so run, not as uncertainly; so fight I, not as one that beateth the air: But I keep under my body, and bring it into subjection: lest that by any means, when I have preached to others, I myself should be a castaway."**

This is definitely not an easy race. It demands total commitment, determination and strength. God's grace is there for us to see us through this race. We need to be immersed in God's Word to be able to run this kind of a race. In this race he said, we have to train to win the prize. When we wait upon God we enter this training of knowing Him. We are humbled and our eyes focus solely to Him for provision in our material and spiritual needs.

One of my sons plays football and he is always speaking about stamina. He is careful about what he eats and he does a lot of training. Many times he asks us to come and watch him. He is proud of his performance. He wears the correct football kit for training and matches. The Word of God is for training. How do we train? We emulate sportsmen.

We train by doing our spiritual exercises, allocating time to read the Bible, praying for ourselves and others, doing what the Bible instructs us and so on. As Christians, the world watches us although we haven't invited them to. They want to see if we keep up to what we preach and any slight mistake is blown out of proportion because we vowed to be in this race.

It is no use cramming verses in the head with no transformation. The Bible uses the words heart and mind interchangeably like in Hebrews 8:10 when God says that He will put His laws on people's minds and write them on their hearts. Memorising verses in the head only means believing the facts in the Bible without the dedication in the heart or mind for spiritual transformation. This is why we need to ask our helper the Holy Spirit to quicken the Word in our hearts so that we are transformed into the mind of Christ. That is the whole essence of reading the Bible for training.

> **"Forasmuch as ye are manifestly declared to be the epistle of Christ ministered by us, written not with ink, but with the Spirit of the living God; not in tables of stone, but in fleshy tables of the heart." (2 Corinthians 3:3)**

We are an epistle, a letter of Christ written on the heart. The Word of God will train us through the Holy Spirit, to deliver the message in the letter in our hearts. Watch what you say and how you behave, then set it with the standard of God and see what God is saying to you and what message you are delivering to others about the letter He wrote on your heart. Your fruit will tell you whether your letter is the one from the Spirit of the living God or from a different spirit.

Let me share with you one wonderful "epistle" I read over ten years ago. I have got a remarkable sister called Jane Dhliwayo. She is naturally gentle, the Lord blessed her with a wonderful loving husband John and they have brilliant respectful children and grandchildren. My sister had never told me in person what her secret was of having all her act together like that. One day she visited us at our home in Hatfield, Harare. Early the next morning around five I felt some movement and I sleepily opened my eyes. I saw sister Jane kneeling down and praying. I was gobsmacked, to say the least. I asked myself why on earth anyone, who seemed to have everything for that matter, wanted to disturb her sleep, to pray. Then it dawned on me that, the life she was enjoying, was a product of her rigorous training in the Word of God. That was the most wonderful epistle I ever read. It inspired me so much that I asked the Lord to give me the courage, to leave my warm blankets for a talk with Him, to train me to humble myself in His presence even when there was nothing I needed. My request was granted.

Some letters are dreadful to open. Letters like bills are not pleasant. We read letters from some people's actions that appear like bills. One day my brother went for an evening prayer meeting and needed a lift from one of the elders. He decided to nudge her before she opened her eyes in prayer, lest she forgot. The elder vehemently turned back and shouted on top of her voice "can't you see I am still praying!" I honestly felt the purpose of her prayer was defeated by her actions. In our eyes she was praying but when pressed she spilled out what was in the heart. This is why our prayer should be to ask God to train us and create in us a clean heart, and then when pressed, it will pour nothing but the consistent love of God which conquers everything. If we train with the Spirit of the living God we will present a pleasant letter with a true reflection of God's disciples.

We are racing with an aim to win, not aimlessly, not to please others, not to be part of a certain group but to win. We are also fighting to win the battle. The Bible is useful for training, whether we consider it a race or war, we need training. The army trains before they can go into war. The Bible will train us to build spiritual muscles of faith, to eat its healthy spiritual food regularly and to exercise our perseverance.

In our spiritual war we are told what the correct kit to wear is, in Ephesians 6:14-17. We are fighting a spiritual war therefore we need spiritual training. We need the Word of God to remain in our hearts. We need the FULL armour on a daily basis. If we leave the helmet then the devil will attack the head, if we leave the belt of truth the devil will incite us to tell lies that day. Imagine going in a muddy field with flip flops. The wise thing would be to take Wellingtons. The wise thing in the spiritual war is to wear the full proper armour with shoes of Good News of peace. Every piece has its purpose and we are not to choose only the one appealing to us and ignore the rest. Choosing one gives the devil the opportunity to penetrate and we fall. His aim is to make us fall not to stand as Paul tells the Ephesians. The Bible is there to train us to do all this in the Lord. Before we go about with our daily chores, it is important to ask the Holy Spirit to clothe us with the full armour.

The Word of God will train us to make a good start, to keep on the track focusing on the prize. Although there are many of us running, only those who trained and abided by the Word of God will win the prize. We do not stop along the track or give up because we are tired. In fighting we also advance in might and power. With the Word of God in us we will run and not grow weary. The Holy Spirit our helper will be with us in the race and in this war to supply the energy and strength. We do not carry along any heavy burdens for the Bible trains us to cast all our cares on the Lord.

> **"Not as though I had already attained, either were already perfect: but I follow after, if that I may apprehend that for which also I am apprehended of Christ Jesus. Brethren, I count not myself to have apprehended: but this one thing I do, forgetting those things which are behind, and reaching forth unto those things which are before," (Philippians 3:12-13).**

The key in this race is pressing on. We do not dwell on the past. Nothing will separate us from the love of God. He will see us through even when those cheering us stop clapping and shouting. We ask for God's unfailing love to help us press on. There are no short cuts in the Bible during training. Our coach, the Lord Jesus Christ went through tribulations for our sake. He knows what it is to suffer and he will train us through the Word for a fulfilling life. We will meet challenges but we have the Bible that guarantees us full training to enable us to conquer all challenges and obstacles.

The Bible trains us to emulate winners and to run the race load free. Burdens hinder our performance in this race.

> **"Wherefore seeing we also are compassed about with so great a cloud of witnesses, let us lay aside every weight, and the sin which doth**

> **so easily beset us, and let us run with patience the race that is set before us." (Hebrews 12:1)**

The great cloud of witnesses is referring to people who lived by faith. Their actions are a paradigm of Christian life. I enjoy reading testimonies. They help me to draw strength from other people's victories and learn from their mistakes. Training with practical experiences of other witnesses helps me to move on watchfully, looking for a new door when God closes another, admitting mistakes and failures, regarding the failures as a lesson well learnt and which I would endeavour not repeat again. The admission releases me from the chains of bondage that impede my race. In training I strive to lay aside every weight and sin because they are the ones that ensnare and slow me down in the race.

I like job adverts which say "no previous experience required, full training will be provided". This is a chance for anyone looking for work. There is a chance for everyone in God's Kingdom. No previous experience is required either. The Word of God provides full training for all ages anywhere.

Those that wait upon the Lord, wait upon the Word for teaching, reproof, correcting and for instruction, not for information but for transformation. They shall be blessed with obedience (**Psalm 119:9-11**), revelation (**1 Corinthians 2:6-14**) and permanent sustenance (**Isaiah 40:8**).

# DAILY WORD OF VICTORY

Then said Jesus to those Jews which believed on him, If ye continue in my word, then are ye my disciples indeed; And ye shall know the truth, and the truth shall make you free.

John 8:31-32

This is my comfort in my affliction: for thy word hath quickened me.

Psalm 119:50

Sanctify them through thy truth: thy word is truth

John 17:17

NOTES:

# Chapter 6
# RENEW STRENGTH

*No God, no strength. Know God, know strength.*

We are challenged to wait so that God can renew our strength. The term *renew* signifies making new again, restoring, extending and starting anew. That is what Isaiah quiet clearly said God would do to those who wait upon Him. If you brave waiting upon Him at your worst state, God is faithful enough to give you the strength to see you through to the next season. At that time when you feel tired, broken, confused and absolutely depleted of strength and energy, God intervenes with His mercies. Even if the situation seems like an insurmountable problem, God is bigger than all situations. When you experience opposition, feel conquered, trapped and you think you have tried hard enough, it is time to review whose strength you are using.

In God you surrender and wait for Him to renew your strength. You rest in His arms in total trust. You put your requests in the *in* basket and trust that the file is being dealt with while you rejoice and pray in thanksgiving. You do not expend your own efforts on the matter because that is our Lord's part.

**Lamentations 3:22-23** says **"It is of the LORD's mercies that we are not consumed, because his compassions fail not. They are new every morning: great is thy faithfulness."** The love of God is steadfast, it never ceases, His mercies never come to an end; they are new every morning and His faithfulness is great. Have you ever feared that the following day the sun might not rise, that maybe it might not set? That is because we trust in God's faithfulness. That is the kind of fearless trust we ought to put on His provision of strength when we think we have reached the end of the rope. Paul says when he is weak that is when he is strong because God's grace is always enough to carry us through.

God does not randomly give us loads of grace when we want it, but he gives us sufficient when we need it. Paul says that he will boast of all the more gladly about his weaknesses, so that Christ's power may rest upon him.

> **"And he said unto me, My grace is sufficient for thee: for my strength is made perfect in weakness. Most gladly therefore will I rather glory in my infirmities, that the power of Christ may rest upon me. Therefore I take pleasure in infirmities, in reproaches, in**

**necessities, in persecutions, in distresses for Christ's sake: for when I am weak, then am I strong." (2 Corinthians 12:9-10)**

### *Seek God earnestly for strength*

Seek the one who gives you strength. Be planted in His Word and you will yield fruits in due season. Ask God to reveal to you what He has assigned you to do. Pray that the Holy Spirit will lead you to the Word that covers your situation. Claim your health now, claim your success, in fact, claim restoration for everything the devil has stolen from you. Seek God earnestly and regain your strength. Again and again the Word of God reminds us that the fight is not ours, the strength is God's. We are advised to wait, to be still, to believe and to stand. He takes over the battle while we are in these positions. It might not be perceptible but that's because we do not fight in flesh.

> **"Finally, my brethren, be strong in the Lord, and in the power of his might. Put on the whole armour of God, that ye may be able to stand against the wiles of the devil. For we wrestle not against flesh and blood, but against principalities, against powers, against the rulers of the darkness of this world, against spiritual wickedness in high places. Wherefore take unto you the whole armour of God, that ye may be able to withstand in the evil day, and having done all, to stand." (Eph 6:10-13).**

This scripture is teaching us that the day of evil will come. The day of evil is inevitable. It came since the fall of man and it will still come today. There is nothing we can do in our power to stop it coming but there is something we can do to endure it – we turn to God and wait upon Him for the next step.

The word "finally" means at the end, after we have said and done everything. God is interested in the final result of what we do. We find that at the end is the time when we are most tired and weakest, after we have done the race, after we have completed our fasting, after we have waited long enough, that is when we should be strong? God is interested in the end product. How we began and what we did in between is inconsequential. The end is what counts and we must be strong with the shield of faith in a defending us.

We do not retreat but we stand firm. This could be the reason why the full armour of God in Ephesians 6 does not offer anything to cover our backs. We are not expected to turn back in trials and run away. We stand rooted in faith, carrying along all the benefits of faith – pleasing God and when we please Him we become blessed and when we are blessed we bless others.

> **"But without faith it is impossible to please him: for he that cometh to God must believe that he is, and that he is a rewarder of them that diligently seek him." (Hebrews 11:6)**

God rewards those who seek Him earnestly, who want to have a relationship with Him, those who want to know Him not *about* Him. Many a time we search the Holy Bible to gather information *about* God and we go to church, maybe share the Word yet we are devoid of that very purpose of reading the Bible, to know Him for our transformation, to become more like Christ. We used to call it missing the Word by 18 inches that is about the distance from the brain to the heart. This means we will have memorised it in the head and the heart remains untransformed. When we seek Him earnestly we acquire the correct gear we need to don for the storms as we wait for God's strength.

### *Not our own strength*

**"….. Not by might, nor by power, but by my spirit, saith the LORD of hosts." (Zechariah 4:6).** Use your own strength and sure enough you shall faint but those that wait upon the Lord shall have their strength renewed by the power of the Holy Spirit.

Strength comes from nourishment. Our nourishment is the Word of God.

> **"For the word of God is quick, and powerful, and sharper than any two edged sword, piercing even to the dividing asunder of soul and spirit, and of the joints and marrow, and is a discerner of the thoughts and intents of the heart." (Hebrews 4:12).**

As I said in the previous chapter, the Word is our life. The Word of God is quick means it is living and active. When anything living and active is planted and nurtured, it grows. The Word grows in good conditions, good intentions, good motives, regular application and faith. It is living and active, therefore when it grows in these good conditions it will produce fruits. It nourishes the weary.

The Word bears the fruits desired by the seed maker who is our God Almighty. When we are strengthened, we produce fruits and fruits are the intended results that we are waiting for. It is sharper than a two edged sword. This means it is going to operate on our hearts dealing with sin, smoothly and with precision. The Word will reveal the truth about God and us otherwise we would not know what and how to ask from the Father if we do not know Him and His promises. It will judge our thoughts and intentions because nothing is hidden from God. The nourishing Word will cut through where we can't see meaning that it will deal with the innermost man, even fighting for us in war fares we are not aware of.

God commanded us to be strong. We just have to ask Him for that strength and its renewal as He promised.

> **"Have not I commanded thee? Be strong and of a good courage; be not afraid, neither be thou dismayed: for the LORD thy God is with thee whithersoever thou goest." (Joshua 1:9).**

We can not do without the guidance and sustenance of the Word of God. That is where all instructions of our spiritual living are carefully laid and explained. It is our spiritual diet. James 1:21-25 implores us to not only read it but be doers of the Word, doers who listen to the voice of the shepherd. This takes us to an important step of being joyful to gain strength.

## *The joy of the Lord is our strength*

It is hard to rejoice in the Lord in times of trouble. We mourn or murmur. We are to rejoice in the Lord always.... (**Philippians 4:4**) verse 6 encourages us further to pray and not be anxious, to give thanks while praying. It is an ultimate test of faith, to have joy and to give thanks in everything even during trials.

The moment we accepted Jesus Christ as our Lord and saviour, we were given the power to become God's children, therefore every promise in the Bible applies to us. The joy of the Lord is when we concede that we have the same authority and power promised in the Bible. Joy is claiming that the blessings of Abraham are ours, goodness and mercy will follow us, that we are not tails but heads that our homes are blessed, our families are blessed, our friends are blessed, our jobs are blessed, our ministries are blessed, our health is blessed and our decisions are blessed! We need to wait upon Him, in His will, and He will renew our strength. He watches over us, He does not sleep nor slumber.

**Nehemiah 8:10** tells us that the joy of the Lord is our strength. Do not allow the enemy to steal your joy. He knows with joy you get strength, with strength you fight the good fight of faith and with faith you receive the grace of God. He will try to steal that joy of going through fire and not getting burnt, the joy of going through the rivers, and not drowning, the joy of waking up every morning in thanksgiving knowing that in due season you get your restoration.

That joy is the strength we need, not the strength from anyone or anything that we see on earth. Joy is derived from a powerful prayer, from the strength of the Word of God, the blood of Jesus and the Holy Spirit. That joy is the strength that sustains us while waiting, while we get renewed, while we walk through the darkest valley of our life in anticipation of rising up the mountain into his marvellous light. Do not allow satan to steal that joy in the vision you have, the joy in that desire in you, in the hope you are holding on to, in your dream or your will power to stay focused on God. Strength, joy and praise are interwoven.

> **"The LORD is my strength and my shield; my heart trusted in him, and I am helped: therefore my heart greatly rejoiceth; and with my song will I praise him."(Psalms 28:7)**

God inhabits in the praises of His people. As we praise Him, He dwells in us and we experience the fullness of His joy and love for us. While we praise and worship Him, tears are replaced with joy, the joy which the Bible says is our strength. The one in us is greater than he that is in the world. Put the situation in God's safe hands and believe that He will lift you up and restore your joy by His strength.

### *Whose voice do you listen to?*

When we submit to God's voice we do His will and He renews our strength. I have learnt that voice recognition is not an overnight or automatic occurrence. I need to have heard the voice several times before I can recognise it. In front of our garden there is a huge green area where all our children in the Estate play together when the weather is fine. Within the numerous screams and shouting, I am able to distinguish my children's voices from the others with accuracy. I believe God does the same when His children call out to Him and I believe God equally wants us to distinguish His voice from any others that tell us what to do. We can only achieve this by seeking sound communication with Him, the way we would recognise someone's voice at the end of the line on the phone.

If we speak to our Father regularly, and develop a strong relationship with Him, we will know His voice. Only His hand can deliver us from being deceived by the devil's voice. God's Word trains us to hear His command. When we wait we might despair and the devil, who Jesus called the father of lies, can shout and convince us that we will never achieve what we are waiting for, that the problem is too big for divine intervention, that waiting is for someone else, that waiting is too uncertain and our matter is more pressing, that we can find another easy solution and repent later, that we can manipulate the situation to speed up the results, that our faith is not strong enough for that kind of waiting or even that the kind of favour we are waiting for occurs only to certain people. The secret lies in discerning and knowing the voice of the one you believe in.

The devil prowled in my life one day. He lied to me and almost convinced me that miracles do not happen anymore. The reason it sounded convincing was because I listened to his voice then went on to ponder and I asked myself how many miracles I had seen lately. That was judgemental. I do not know why I was looking for more miracles yet I just had to look at myself breathing, my children playing, my family and friends nearby and witness the miracle of life. They, including myself are unique miracles of life. I repented immediately, calling unto the voice of life, the Word of God.

The devil has a loud voice. He will tell you that so and so did it without waiting on the Lord' strength and they are now even better than you, that whatever you are trying to do is useless and you will not finish it, that you have not been called to do what you are doing, that God is punishing you that is why you are in that storm, therefore He is not a fair God, that you are a looser, but guess what – it is all lies. The devil shouts, but the Holy Spirit whispers. The devil is a liar and a deceiver. Listen to the small convicting voice of the Holy Spirit, the one who cleanses and comforts us daily and in times of trouble.

> **"The thief cometh not, but for to steal, and to kill, and to destroy: I am come that they might have life, and that they might have it more abundantly." (John 10:10).**

When I read this verse the only things that came to my mind were physical things being stolen. One time my sister had a problem with her son. We started praying for him. A few days later my other sister also had a problem with her son. We were devastated. My mentor phoned me and gave me the above verse. She told me that the devil wanted to steal our time. Instead of investing all our time on one child, he led the second one into trouble so that our time could be divided into two. She said the devil's sums are division and subtraction and God's sums are multiplication and addition. We continued in united prayer and the Lord answered. Abundant life is what God planned for us. We must proclaim prosperity, victory and healing in every area of our lives. The devil can steal the knowledge you have about God's providence but pray always for the Holy Spirit to help you discern God's voice to gain strength.

The enemy instils fear but fear is not from God, he roars like a lion but he is not a lion. We were given a spirit of power and a sound mind no matter what the devil says. He will put obstacles in your way to trip you but God will lift you up. He will throw a blanket of doubt on you and you begin to think "what if..." What if this is the wrong route, what if the answer does not come on time, what if this fails, and what if it wasn't God......God's timing is perfect timing, listen for His voice. His way is the best way, His strength is everlasting. As long as it is within His plan, as long as He takes you to it, He will see you through it. Discern His voice, obey and get your strength renewed.

## *Listen to the Shepherd's voice*

It is amazing how when a disaster strikes everyone around you suddenly becomes an expert, "you should have done this and you shouldn't have done that". People fret around you confusing you with contradicting advice. This is when you are vulnerable, when your hope is flickering and you are tempted to try anything to survive. This is the time when you, as a child of God should not turn to self pity or expect strong supporting arms from people. Listen to the voice of the Shepherd.

The Bible says:

> **"And David was greatly distressed; for the people spake of stoning him, because the soul of all the people was grieved, every man for his sons and for his daughters: but David encouraged himself in the LORD his God." 1 Sam 30:6**

David encouraged HIMSELF in the Lord. David did not trust in men, in his power, in his wealth or in his own understanding but in the Lord. David was distressed. Saul wanted to kill him. The army he joined rejected him. The place he called home was burnt and his family was taken away. His fellow men worsened it by planning to stone him. That is a breaking point. Remarkably he did not beg anyone. He knew where to turn to, whose voice to listen to. He made a good choice and asked for direction from God. God told him to pursue them and he won.

In storms such as these, we need to know who to turn to and whose voice to obey. We need to read between the lines and decipher the fine print of spiritual living. Naturally we have the tendency of rushing for the spectacular and missing the miraculous. We begin to wonder whether it is God, the devil or us speaking. Jesus says "My sheep hear my voice, and I know them, and they follow me:" (John 10:27).

We have a couple in the leadership who lifted me a step higher in listening to the voice of the shepherd – Ruth and Fanuel Zendera. They have drilled and hammered a clear message that only the Shepherd knows what is best for His sheep. Although we were aware of it somehow when disaster struck many voices spoke and we lost track. One day the devil tried his tricks and brought one catastrophe after another. One aunt got detained, her sister broke her leg, one of my sons had his phone snatched by a gang, all in a space of hours. I was numb with fear and confusion but I thank God for Mr and Mrs Zendera, who are ever there to bring sanity in situations like these. They help people carry their burdens by refocusing them to the cross. They prayed with us, gave us the Word to rely on and told us to listen to God's voice only. We prayed and in less than a week God had answered, aunt was released, the other one was healing and my son found reassurance in God. They reminded us that although we had solicitors, Doctors and Counsellors we had to be still and listen first to God's voice in our discouragement before making any move.

One warning they always give us is to be careful of only listening to His voice in times of trouble then ignoring it any other time. Mr Zendera says in his village they have a small river which derived its name from its nature of getting full only when it rains. At that moment he says, it is so powerful that it drags logs, animals and anything in its way. After a few hours after the rains it subsides so low you won't believe it is the same river that had been roaring with power. He warns us not to have that kind of attitude in God, getting zealous only when we have problems or during preaching. The voice of the Shepherd should be a continuous sound in our hearts. We should allow it to give us a constant flow of power and if it does overflow during preaching, praise the Lord for the bonus, but we should not allow any ebbing or decline afterwards.

Pray for the Spirit of discernment to differentiate voices as the devil can use the same vessel God uses, I will explain this below. Without the spirit of discernment anything that comes your way is going to sound Godly. Only a closer walk with God, can assure the elimination of doubting who is speaking. Different advices will be offered, even good advice but not all good advice is God advice.

Examine the following incidents and see how crucial the Spirit of discernment is in our lives. In the same book of 1 Samuel in chapter 26 the same man David went into Saul's camp with Abishai. We know Saul wanted to kill David. They found Saul sleeping with his spear near him. Notice how Abishai mentions God as the one who had put Saul in their hands! It was good advice, but not God advice. David recognised that the message was not from God. He did not listen to Abishai he saved his enemy's life. Although he was not glorifying what Saul was doing, he knew Saul was wrong, but he preferred to listen to God's command, that of not touching the anointed one of God. Abishai offered to slay Saul himself, which means David could have been exonerated from the crime, but David was committed to doing that which was right in the eyes of the Lord. How often do we get tempted to go ahead with a wrong plan just because we will not be proven guilty? That is not God advice, listen to the voice of the Shepherd.

In Matthew 16:22 after Jesus had spoken of His death we find Peter telling Him what I feel most of us could have said. He felt that Jesus as their King should not die. That was good advice in flesh. But Jesus discerned the spirit behind him. He told the devil get behind him. Not dying was not the will of God. Listen to the voice of the shepherd and know his voice for certain. He is there in the storm and without total commitment you might miss His voice.

In Acts 16 Paul and Silas are followed by a slave girl who shouts that they are real servants of God. That was true but the spirit which made the girl speak was a spirit of divination and Paul cast it out. The spirit of discernment is at the core of our waiting while we are in these debilitating situations. Jesus promised us a helper who can teach us to discern.

The two men were flogged severely and thrown into jail but at midnight they sang and prayed. This is beyond human valour! They should be in pain, whining or even murmuring to God but they are singing, praising and praying! The result is as astounding as their actions. There is a tremor, the prison foundations are shaken and the doors open. They did not listen to the slave girl; they knew the voice of the Shepherd.

If we listen to God's voice, and obey His commands He will make a way in the wilderness and a river in the desert. The ridiculous becomes the miraculous while you are in the storm. The storm imprisons us but in praise and prayer, we hear His voice and the storm shall be shaken to nothing. In dark hours God speaks to us and reveals to us who He really is. In that prison you find yourself locked today, in that prison of debts, illness, controversy, defeat or hopelessness, with your wounds from these floggings, which song are you singing? Who are you calling now? Whose voice are you listening to? There is a Living God, the one that Peter and Silas praised in prison, Who is waiting for you right now to help you in your situation. Call unto Him now, listen to His voice and believe while you are praying that He has heard you, and victory will be yours.

Our Shepherd the Lord Jesus Christ is the Way the Truth and the Life. At His name every knee should bow, in heaven and on earth and under the earth, and every tongue should confess that He is Lord. Only His voice should reign in our hearts. God exalted Him to the highest place and was given the name that is above every name therefore no other voice can silence His. The Holy Spirit, our helper and our counsellor will help us discern the voice of the Shepherd. He is the Spirit of wisdom and understanding, the spirit of grace, of holiness and eternity. Call Him and He will impart discernment to you and the Good Shepherd will lead you to green pastures for strength.

# DAILY WORD OF VICTORY

It is God that girdeth me with strength, and maketh my way perfect.

Psalm 18:32

God is our refuge and strength, a very present help in trouble.

Psalm 46.1

The adversaries of the LORD shall be broken to pieces; out of heaven shall he thunder upon them: the LORD shall judge the ends of the earth; and he shall give strength unto his king, and exalt the horn of his anointed.

1Sam 2.10

# Chapter 7
# MOUNT UP IN STORMS

*Each storm contains a new definition of trusting God*

Mounting up on wings like an eagle brings visions of majesty, magnificence, force, vision, strength determination etc. We usually forget to imagine the warfare of mounting against a storm, which is what the eagle often does. Maybe you are in a storm today, a storm of unpleasant challenges but let me tell you something, if you wait on Him, He shall renew your strength and you shall mount up on wings like an eagle.

Whichever storm you are facing today bear in mind you are not alone. Storms have no formula or a trusted theory at all, they are unpreventable, they can come incessantly and unabated but be assured that they can not overcome you in the face of the Lord who said"....**In the world ye shall have tribulation: but be of good**

**cheer; I have overcome the world." (John 16:33)** They come for a purpose and God is there to see us through these hard times. Storms are the substance that can test what kinds of trees we are and only a good tree brings forth good fruit.

Let us bear in mind what I have said before about "thy will be done". If you are going to mount up on wings in your spiritual life, be prepared to face the storm with the knowledge that God strengthens us. Let us say then that you ask God to give you more love, more patience or more faith. In response to the request God allows you to go through a trying period to facilitate their development. You encounter obstacles and resistance along the way. How do you stem the tide? Is your aim to be moulded by God into what He wants in His way or you would rather prefer to try to dodge trials as much as possible yet still hope to be transformed? I have known many people who have chosen to be mediocre in their prayer life in fear of encountering storms. They think being prayer warriors puts them at risk but they fail to consider how riskier it would be to live a prayer less life. Fear will not eliminate the storms from your life anyhow. Fear only makes the situation worse by intimidating you into believing that you are defeated yet you have a greater person in you than he that is in the world.

When mounting up, we do not rely on our own wisdom or strength, we lean on God. Mighty men of God, like Paul who were doing God's will and Job a man who was righteous in the eyes of God had various storms in their lives despite doing God's will. God sustained them. These are the hardest times to seek and trust Him. Our decisions in difficulties determine whether our faith will move the mountain or we take the back seat and the mountain moves our faith.

Suffering is the brush which polishes us for perseverance, character and hope to manifest. It strengthens our wings for take off into soaring. It removes all the impurities to reveal the inner beauty in us. Storms make us mount up where we have never been before. If we are obedient to wait on the Lord, this is the time He reveals certain things to us, He tests us, teaches us, cleanses and refines us and He turns our focus from all else to Him. We depend on God's Word to do the work in us, to mould us into the image of Christ. The Word prepares us. God is the potter and we are the clay (**Isaiah 64:8**) and mounting up on wings is one way of being moulded. **2 Timothy 2:20** tells us that we are different vessels for different uses. This is why we should not try to be like somebody else but the person who God wants to mould us into according His intended purpose and use in His Kingdom. Mounting up on wings entails obedience the God's calling, and willingness to perform within the boundaries of the moulded vessel. Ask the Holy Spirit to reveal your calling.

Here are some of the ways storms can mould us and make us mount up on wings like an eagle.

## *Protecting us*

In some instances suffering is allowed to protect us. When a job offer is turned down it sounds horrible but it could be protection from unforeseen future problems within the company. You might even get fired as a way of God turning your attention to a new door of a mightier opportunity that He has opened for you. When you fail to relocate at your planned time, take heart maybe your business, ministry, job or family was meant to flourish where you are. In fact what we might regard as a failure, could be God's hand protecting us and we need to confirm it with Him, the author and the finisher of our lives.

In **Numbers 22-24** there is an account of the prophet Balaam who made God angry and went on His donkey to King Balak. The angel of the Lord came three times and the donkey could see it but Balaam was blind to it. The donkey swerved making Balaam angry. He beat it until it spoke to him. When God let him see the angel with a sword, he was told that if the donkey had not swerved he could have been killed. God can make our situations swerve to save us from imminent death or harm. He calls us to do something and in the process we are blind to certain things. These are also times we might think that we were probably not called to pursue it in the first place. But seek God and see what the *donkey* is seeing.

One day we were called to go and comfort a friend who had lost a sister-in-law. The lady who was supposed to lead the way left before we did and we made our own convoy. Everything that could go wrong that day went wrong. We got stuck in heavy traffic, my indicators failed all of a sudden and an accident was imminent. We got lost and the satellite navigator we were using made us turn in circles .

The Pastor and his wife were supposed to go and pray for another family in a different area. It took us over an hour where it normally takes ten minutes to manoeuvre from the main street to the other side and by then we were relying on mobiles to find out where each car was. I had forgotten to tell my husband where we were going as it is our custom to update each other on every move. He was frantically trying to get in touch with me on a mobile that was engaged by others who were lost. The Pastor and his wife eventually made a u-turn and went to minister with the family in the other area. When they got there the matter was more pressing than they had envisaged and God intervened in a mighty way. We proceeded with our plan and we comforted this lady with a powerful message from one of the speakers.

Later on as we discussed the trip some were convinced we had been taken for a ride by the devil but I was given a different revelation that God wanted us to divide into two groups for the work of God to proceed simultaneously. Maybe if we had gone to one place it would have been too late for the Pastor to travel to the couple. As a result the couple might have been adversely affected. We easily become frustrated like Balaam and we blame satan for our misfortunes when maybe, it is in fact God trying to tell us something. If Balaam had sought the Lord at that time, he might have known he was being protected. Whenever you find yourself in a situation where everything seems to be going from bad to worse, take time to focus on God and see if you need to rebuke the devil or thank God for His protection or leading.

## *Strengthening our faith and patience*

The work I do determines the reward I get. The same applies to the faith I place in God's providence in hard times, it will determine the amount of patience I gain at the end of the season. God wants us to have a good and pleasant attitude in storms, exercising our faith. If we persevere, our faith and patience grow.

God is full of compassion and mercy and He is faithful enough to hear us when we pray in faith.

> **"And not only so, but we glory in tribulations also: knowing that tribulation worketh patience; And patience, experience; and experience, hope: And hope maketh not ashamed; because the love of God is shed abroad in our hearts by the Holy Ghost which is given unto us. For when we were yet without strength, in due time Christ died for the ungodly. For scarcely for a righteous man will**

> **one die: yet peradventure for a good man some would even dare to die. But God commendeth his love toward us, in that, while we were yet sinners, Christ died for us."** (Romans 5:3-5)

We need a strong free will to let go and let God have His way. It does not matter what the source of the storm you are facing today is. Whether its a result of what you have done or said, whether it is someone's doing or it has been allowed by God to call you back to Him, to test you or to make you grow in Him, the only important thing to remember is that no storm is without purpose. No storm is stronger than God either. If we wait upon Him in faith He will safely deliver us by His grace. We learn to depend, focus and trust more on Him during the troubles. We become aware of His presence and control. We grow stronger in faith and patience and we soar like eagles. We experience something supernatural – peace in the face of calamities.

His Word says:

> **"My brethren, count it all joy when ye fall into divers temptations; Knowing this, that the trying of your faith worketh patience. But let patience have her perfect work, that ye may be perfect and entire, wanting nothing."** (James 1:2-4).

Turn your mind away from "why" and focus on "what" you will become at the end of the stormy season. Consider it pure joy because we all want to be strong one way or the other. In medication we look for the strongest. We look for food that gives us the best nutrients. We all want the best schools for our children and so on. Get up and act in the storm. Finish that work He began in you. Follow that dream. Answer that calling. Respond to what the inner voice of God is saying. Storm or no storm, move on. Exercise your faith and it will not fail to grow stronger.

God does wonders during storms. He enables us to take some time and reshuffle our timetables and priorities. If the storm is going to come anyway then why not take the more beneficial side of waiting upon Him in joy and gain strength for endurance in the hardship. This verse says patience must finish its work. That confirms that there should be some activity in our lives while we are in the valley. When its work is perfect, meaning when it is complete, when it finishes its work, we become mature and we lack nothing for we will have learnt who the source is and what we need to do in times of need.

Patience is a fruit of the spirit (Galatians 5:22), which will grow in a storm. Patience is not determined by how long we wait but by having a good attitude while waiting. Patience bears longsuffering, endurance and perseverance. Its perfect work sifts out impurities leaving a purified character.

We had a new house and in the back garden we decided to grow vegetables. When we started digging I was amazed at the amount of rubbish we unearthed. There were burnt mattresses, bottles, cans, you name it. It looked like a dumping place. A few days later after a lot of work, it was perfect for planting. We still pick up one or two things but most of the ground is clean.

That is what the Holy Spirit does to make us bear fruit. He removes anger, hatred, grudges and many negative items to make our hearts clean in order to plant the fruit of the Spirit which lives within us. That is why the psalmist in Psalms 139:23 says "search me Lord...". The Holy Spirit will search and unearth things that might even surprise you. You could have forgotten them but if you ask in truth, He will bring them out and help you deal with them.

We are "**Strengthened with all might, according to his glorious power, unto all patience and longsuffering with joyfulness; (Colossians 1:11)**" God's promise in the storm will be fulfilled through the fruit of patience. It states *in joyfulness*, not in murmuring, in idleness or in complaining, regardless of circumstances. "**For ye have need of patience, that, after ye have done the will of God, ye might receive the promise" (Hebrews 10:36).** This fruit of the spirit can only develop when we put our trust in God and walk in the spirit. Compare the patience you had before and the one after the storm. Like all valuable commodities, patience is often scarce in us and only the doers of the Word will possess it.

## *Lifting us up and depending on God*

If it is temptation that is throwing us in the storm, the Word of God says in **1 Corinthians 10:13** that we will be given enough grace to withstand temptation and God will not let us be tempted more than we can bear.

Temptation brings storms. If we yield to it we fall but if we turn to God and resist the devil, he will flee. God will provide a way out for us and we can bear it and He will lift us up. We undergo pruning in this process of passing through a dark valley. Victory in one storm through God's strength, equips us spiritually for the next one. You know who to trust even though the enemy might try to make it worse for **"When the enemy shall come in like a flood, the Spirit of the LORD shall lift up a standard against him." Isaiah 59:19(b)**

We grow in the Lord and whatever the enemy puts in our way the Lord will lift a standard against him. He might try the same trick all the time or he might play on your weakness but in all circumstances go back to the one who is, among other names, the Redeemer, (Isaiah 59:20), the Helper (Hebrews 13:6) and the Refuge from the storm (Isaiah 25:4). I now know that the devil is an expert in people's weaknesses. He can come through your partner and make you fight. He can come through your child and make them wild, through your best friend, through work and so on. We can conquer by asking God to lift us up and set us free.

When we are carried up in the storm we reach out for the hand of God. His Hand is pushed by prayer and He will lift us up to safety and give us the peace which surpasses all understanding. If we are in His will, have faith, reading His Word and doing it, praying with the right motive, we are guaranteed to fly on wings like eagles to a place of peace. The Word of God declares that the Name of the Lord is a strong tower, the righteous run into it and they are safe. The storm still rages below but God has lifted us up high enough in a place where it will not affect us. That is why it is vital to pray while we are still in the storm for after that current dies down, the power to lift our wings up has also died down. This can force us to stay down, quit trusting in God or fail to request enough strength to follow Christ.

That does not mean that God does not hear a prayer when we are not in trouble. He always does. But after the ravages of a storm amidst the rubble of confusion, despair, hurt, pain and grief, it is harder to find the insight of where to start from let alone the courage to rise up again. The way we search scripture, pray and fast when we are faced with a storm is different. It is deeper, more determined and more focused. Sometimes it even yields more fruit because we search the Word with a goal, waiting in anticipation for an outcome. It becomes a more earnest and intimate relationship, different from our usual daily prayer and Bible study. **Hebrews 12:3** exhorts us not to be weary. **"For consider him that endured such contradiction of sinners against himself, lest ye be wearied and faint in your minds."**

We learn to depend on Him even if it does not suit us or does not appear attractive. Depending on God in a storm becomes hardest when we try to figure out our own solutions. If they work then, rest assured they will be short lived and we will be running back to Him. We fail because we are living in a society of reasoning and theories. But God says we should not be conformed to this world but be transformed by the renewing of our minds (**Romans 12:2**). While the world depends entirely on logic, evidence, frameworks and the like, we are to depend on the One whose ways are higher than our ways. We are in this world but not of this world. This means God is not asking us to be isolated from this world but to be insulated within it. Why should we depend on what a prescription says rather than the creator of the one who made the prescription? Ask the creator to lead the physician to the best prescription. God wants us to totally depend on Him in His own time.

Every situation has a unique challenge on how to deal with it. With the guidance of the Holy Spirit we discern whether the storm requires fasting and for how long, a special offering or solitude where we can have full attention on the Lord. **"And the peace of God, which passeth all understanding, shall keep your hearts and minds through Christ Jesus" (Philippians 4:7)** and **Psalm 57:1** in the second part says **"..yea, in the shadow of thy wings will I make my refuge, until these calamities be overpast."** We will safely rest where God puts us until the calamities have passed. The calamities have not been taken away completely but we find refuge in God and are protected from harm until they are over.

## *Helping others*

Through our Bible study we will learn how to pray fervently, repent and forgive, believe we have received, quoting God's Word in prayer, having a good motive when we ask and so on. God will never leave us nor forsake us. Through our experiences we get the opportunity to help others in similar situations. The onus is on us to surrender to Him who lifts the needy from the dust. We can not depend on God while still holding on to something else, a certain addiction, maybe to food or gambling, too much love of money, laziness, lust or anything sinful in His sight. Whatever we keep holding on to is like a chain that will certainly pull us down and prevent us from flying to that place of rest. We must let go, totally surrender to Him and conform to His Word to enable us to bless others in need.

God blessed Abraham and said he would also be a blessing to others in Genesis 12:3. We often pray for our own blessings and forget to pray to be a blessing to others. Trials sometimes train us so that we also help others who find themselves in the same predicament. In **2 Corinthians 1:3-6** the Bible says:

> **"Blessed be God, even the Father of our Lord Jesus Christ, the Father of mercies, and the God of all comfort; Who comforteth us in all our tribulation, that we may be able to comfort them which are in any trouble, by the comfort wherewith we ourselves are comforted of God. For as the sufferings of Christ abound in us, so our consolation also aboundeth by Christ. And whether we be afflicted, it is for your consolation and salvation, which is effectual in the enduring of the same sufferings which**

> **we also suffer: or whether we be comforted, it is for your consolation and salvation."**

There is no doubt; storms bring forth a good thing if we wait upon the Lord. They all have a purpose. We give what we need. If we need comfort, we comfort others, if we need peace, we make peace with others, and if we need love we give others love and so on.

In Genesis 50:20 Joseph told his brothers that they meant to hurt him but God turned their evil into good. He saved lives but we all know the story of this young man. His brothers were jealous of him. They rejected and sold him. He became a slave in Egypt and his master was Potiphar. Potiphar's wife falsely accused and betrayed Joseph and he was wrongly imprisoned. Joseph was let down many times but all these sufferings and temptations eventually led him to save the lives of many people. Storms can be allowed so that we help and save others.

Have you ever realised that it is when we are "pressed" that our true character comes out? Joseph was over pressed but what was in his heart was nothing but love. The characters we paint at church or in public may not be the real us. Wait until something upsets you and watch what oozes out. Will it be something helpful or destructive? Pressures are good indicators of what is inside our hearts and they help us take the appropriate action at the right time. That way we can proceed to help others.

When we soar up wings, we encounter trials and suffering, we groan in pain but we should avoid mourning. Storms bring transformation for those who wait on the Lord. They bring a new revelation of who our God is each time we are elevated above the storms. We get to know Him better and His Word has a deeper meaning. Obey His commands as you face the storm while soaring. If He tells you to relocate but you regard as a storm because you feel comfortable where you are, obey Him because He knows what is best for you. When a useful bank loan is refused, before you mourn, wait and speak to the One who is greater than the bank Manager first, He might have planned a better financial arrangement for you with less interest. The will of God will never take you where His grace will not protect you. He will certainly lift you up on wings like an eagle.

# DAILY WORD OF VICTORY

For your shame ye shall have double; and for confusion they shall rejoice in their portion: therefore in their land they shall possess the double: everlasting joy shall be unto them.

Isaiah 61:7

Many are the afflictions of the righteous: but the LORD delivereth him out of them all.

Psalm 34:19

Be not deceived; God is not mocked: for whatsoever a man soweth, that shall he also reap.

Galatians 6:7

# Chapter 8
# ON WINGS LIKE AN EAGLE

*Why hang around with chickens when you are an eagle that can fly?*

So far I am sure you have appreciated the value of what Isaiah said about the merits of waiting upon the Lord, inducing renewal of strength to help us mount up. This ushers us into our next promise of soaring on wings like an eagle. Why an eagle and not just fly like a bird? Simply because the qualities of an eagle are special and that's how special our flight will be when we wait upon the Lord. Therefore let us examine the eagle's characteristics to help us get an idea of what we might also encounter during a storm.

The eagle has mighty strength physically. Some of its characteristics are strong talons, stronger than a man's hand. It has such strong eyesight that it has the ability to look straight into the sun. It can see as far as 5 km from the sky. It has strong wings that can prevail against a storm. The eagle builds a strong nest high up on a cliff with thorns and sticks first for outside protection. Then it puts fur from other animals for the comfort of its eaglets. It nurtures the eaglets and trains them out of the nest in due time.

In the face of all the storms of life God will make us fly to a safe place. Now that we are able to renew our strength through waiting we can flap first but because we are in the middle of storms, the storms that made us wait on the Lord in the first place, we are going to glide effortlessly while God sustains us. The eagle waits for storms to take off and it uses the storm force to soar. The strong currents lift it up higher and higher until it is above the storm where it finds comfort.

Although we do not make a deliberate effort to anticipate a storm but when it does come, we use its force to pray and fast earnestly, just the way we would secure more reinforcements before a natural storm. The strength of these prayers will lift us spiritually higher and higher until we have risen above the storm.

Do not wait until the storm is over to start praying and praising God. Pray and praise now, read His Word now, put your faith in Him now for this is the moment when take off is due. Set your wings now and use the storm currents to pick you up and soar to a place of peace. Or else you have to wait for another storm to lift you and help you glide. He is there in the storm just as Jesus was there when the 12 disciples were in the boat on a stormy lake in **Matthew 24:22-33.** He was in the storm in the dark and Peter called out to Him. Call now while the storm is raging. He will calm it and reveal Himself to you. In the process you learn something new, you see Him clearer, He draws closer to you and you draw closer to Him.

### *Build your faith on the rock*

The Bible is very clear about where we should build our faith. **Hebrews 3:4** says that God is the builder of everything and we are the labourers (**1 Corinthians 3:9**). We seek His guidance in this labour of building because we are only there to take instructions on how to build. God will guide us through strong building materials of love, patience, goodness, discipline etc. We are warned that "**Except the LORD build the house, they labour in vain that build it: except the LORD keep the city, the watchman waketh but in vain.**" (**Psalm 127:1**). Our Lord Jesus was a carpenter. He knew the importance of a strong foundation. Jesus taught us how to build sensibly in Matthew 7:24-27:

> **"Therefore whosever heareth these sayings of mine, and doeth them, I will liken him unto a wise man, which built his house upon a rock: And the rain descended, and the floods came, and the winds blew, and beat upon the house; and it fell not: for it was founded upon a rock. And every one that heareth these sayings of mine, and doeth them not, shall be likened unto a foolish man, which built his**

**house upon the sand: And the rain descended, and the floods came, and the winds blew, and beat upon that house; and it fell: and great was the fall of it".**

A foundation is not visible but is the most vital part of the house. Likewise, we might not see what you build your life upon but remember it is the most important part of your life. When storms come they blow every house regardless of the type of foundation. Is your foundation on material stuff or spiritual things? Storm will give the answer. Are you hearing and doing the Word?

The eagle's nest is high up on a rock away from prey. In prayer and in the Word we live high up on our rock the Lord Jesus Christ (**1 Corinthians 10:4**). He is the immovable foundation of our, faith and hope. In Him we find refuge and protection away from our enemies. Once our faith is firmly built on this rock, no enemy will reach us. Winds and storms will come but we shall remain firm on the rock. The eagle does not change the rock on which it builds its nest. It sharpens its beak and claws on the rock for efficient hunting. We remain rooted on our Rock of Salvation, Jesus Christ. We sharpen our swords, the Word, on this Rock Jesus Christ. We do not change from one God to another, for there is only one Living God, the Alpha and the Omega, Our God who does great and unsearchable things. There is no substitute.

While high on the rock we have the opportunity of getting the whole view of what is surrounding us below. We can see what is moving or creeping towards us and we stand prepared. While on Jesus the Rock, the Holy Spirit will impart discernment in us. We will be capable of seeing what is approaching us. We pray in preparation to endure it. How many verses do we memorise per week? How many do we use to defend ourselves from the fiery darts of the devil? Here is a challenge – take out your sword, the Word, from its sheath, use it today, sharpen it on the Rock by obeying what it says and see God working miracles in your life.

### *Focus on the Son for security*

I pointed out that eagles painstakingly put together thorns and sticks to make the nest stable and secure. Then they put fur and any soft material they find. We are still reminded of the material we focus on when building. God wants us to have that security in our lives and His love builds a protective wall around us. We live in hope and assurance that we are free from harm. Even though we shall walk in the valley of the shadow of death, we shall not die for it is merely a shadow. Even though we are facing our enemies, in trials and tribulations, we will come out more than conquerors. **2 Thessalonians 3:3** says that He strengthens us and protects us from evil, **Psalm 91:3-7** says that He will protect us from danger and He is our refuge and fortress, **2 Timothy 4:18** says that He rescues us from evil attacks. The Bible declares God as He who keeps us from falling. We indeed have a plethora of assurances to depend on.

Back to the eagle's strong vision and sight, the eagle is capable of looking straight into the sun. When we wait on the Lord we fly like these eagles, we look straight in the Light of the world, our Lord Jesus Christ (**John 8:12**). We focus on Him not our obstacles until the storm is over. Consider the aim of athletes in a race who I mentioned before, they do not look on those who are cheering. They focus only on the end line. They have sheer determination to win. Our focus is on the Son. Once we diverge, we are prone to noticing those discouragements, hindrances and negative forces around us. We have to emulate the eagle which focuses on the prey until it catches it. Right now, only a season away, your breakthrough, your healing, your victory, that answer you have been waiting for, is at your disposal, if you keep focusing on the Son. Only those who have a not negotiable focus on the Lord will win.

The Bible is laden with promises of protection if we abide in God. We need to proclaim them and focus on the Son for their purposes to prevail. We do not fear bad news for our God is the God of gods. The Bible is pregnant with promises of understanding, wisdom and vision. When we go to the supermarket we are offered points as members of the supermarket's club. Unless we focus on them and redeem them, they will expire and we loose out on offers that were rightfully ours. As members of the body of Christ we ought to focus and redeem those promises or else we loose out on what is rightfully ours.

In **2 Kings 4** there is an amazing story of the Shunamite woman who had a son after Elisha's prophecy. The son had a sudden illness and died unexpectedly. She was undoubtedly devastated but I am intrigued by this woman's focus. She knew God had spoken to His prophet. When she was asked if it was well she responded that all was well. I do not believe anyone doubting God would make such a bold declaration in the midst of such a loss. But for this woman all was well because she focused on God's Word not on the circumstance. I believe if she had shared it with anyone, they would have thought she had lost it. Focusing and trusting entirely on God will raise even the dead situations in your life today. Focus on Him and declare that all is well and witness restoration in your situation.

## *Watch your nest*

God knew us before we were even formed in our mother's womb (**Jeremiah 1:5**). His aim is to give us a life full of joy, peace and happiness. **"For I know the thoughts that I think toward you, saith the LORD, thoughts of peace, and not of evil, to give you an expected end." (Jeremiah 29:11)** We build our nests in our community, family, friends, church, work etc. Unless the Lord builds them for us, we are building on weak foundations. Consequently when storms come we will collapse. The Lord watches us grow gradually. He will not expect us to do mighty things when we are still young, or to be inundated with the comfort of material things while immature but God expects us to grow and develop. He wants us to seek Him first and progress. He does not want us to remain infants in nappies. He wants us to be weaned. He knows our needs at every stage, even in the storm. He is waiting for us to ask for assistance.

Eaglets wait expectantly for food from their mother. We also wait upon the Word for feeding. We go to church and the Pastor feeds the flock. As the eaglet grows the mother shakes the nest to try to make the eaglet get out and learn to fly. We get storms of life from time to time to, among other things; try to shake our comfortable nests to make us grow. God wants to train us to fly on our own. He tries to teach us to feed our souls not only on church days, not only from the Pastor but also in our own endeavour to have personal walk with Him.

If the eaglet resists then the mother starts dismantling the nest, taking off the cushioning stuff and lets the eaglet be pricked. Often this compels it to move out. Likewise if we do not respond to God's command or forsake our Christian walk, He will remove those things we trust in more than Him. Even the Prophet Elijah who was being fed by the ravens and drinking water from the brook had to move on after the ravens were no longer bringing him meat and the brook had dried. We like Elijah should keep listening to the voice of God and depending on Him and including Him at all times in all our plans.

When we exclude God from our plans we build nests with false and illusionary security. To beckon us back God will take away those cushions that distract us from listening, obeying and trusting entirely on Him. That way we become uncomfortable and are nudged to turn back to Him. What is your nest? What is in it? Is it your status, career, power, family, children, friends, pleasure, money, business, job? Whatever you are clinging on to, there where your heart is, that thing which you think you can not do without, is your nest. Comfortable nests are not wrong but ask yourself if it was the Lord who built it or if you are not putting more trust in it than God. If God did not build it or if it is becoming more important than God, then repentance is necessary otherwise you labour in vain.

I used to dread change. If anyone had come to my office they would find my order exactly as it was many years before that. I disliked the effort of making a change to the extent that I preferred living in a small house than moving. I felt comfortable with my same circle of friends, any new ones disturbed me. I was comfortable in the church I attended and I did not want to make any slight movement for seminars, conventions or anything that seemed like an extra curriculum in church. I was cosy in the Sunday Services and could not commit a few minutes alone with the Lord. I had my comfortable nest of procrastination and I intended to keep it that way. When the nest was shaken, I tell you, I sought the Lord with such zeal that even surprised me.

There is absolutely nothing wrong with having that comfortable nest. The problem comes when we adore it more than God and replace Him with it. It is wrong when it makes us trivialise His Word and ignore fellowshipping with Him. If it begins to separate us from the Glory of God, it is wrong. If something were to be removed from our life and we loose our joy in the Lord then it is an indicator that we are placing it in the wrong position in relation to God. We can regret loosing it and miss it but we have to forge on in joy and communion with our God. If we resist God's calling because of the nest, He will stir it.

> **"As an eagle stirreth up her nest, fluttereth over her young, spreadeth abroad her wings, taketh them, beareth them on her wings; so the Lord alone did lead him.." (Deut. 32:11-12).**

Finally, the mother eagle then takes the eaglet from the cliff and drops it. Now that sounds very cruel but watch what it does, before the eaglet hits the ground the mother swoops under it and carries it back. It repeats this exercise until the eaglet has grasped the idea of flying resulting in a well trained, courageous and powerful eaglet. This is where we stand. We are dropped in difficulties for loving and stern training. God won't let us fall and after a while we become stronger in Him. He always lifts us on His wings, of providence, deliverance, exaltation, immeasurable love, faithfulness, mercy and grace before we fall. We begin to experience the magnitude of his everlasting love and care that surpasses knowledge. Ask the Lord to help you scrutinise your nest.

### *Feed on the Word*

An eagle uses its strong talons to lift its food, carry it away and consume it. We ask the Holy Spirit for strong discernment to carry our food which is the Word of

God, into our hearts, meditate on it and do it as already discussed in the preceding chapters. We ask the Holy Spirit for guidance when praying and reading the Bible. He will reveal to us what we need to know. Even when the situation looks hopeless He helps us bear it. The battle is not ours, we have got a great commander and leader who Himself is the Way we are following.

Eagles do not eat dead meat. They only eat their own kill unlike scavengers. Children of God should strive to be in a living Bible believing church, where they are fed God's Word as it is by Spirit filled leaders. We need churches that encourage us not to attend services only for socialising or to get excited by the preaching, but to draw new strength so that we can soar on wings like eagles. The Bible encourages us to gather, to attend church and to share as part of the body of Christ. God wants His children to feed on His fresh, incorruptible, indestructible and everlasting Word. **Jesus said, "... Verily, verily, I say unto you, Except ye eat the flesh of the Son of man, and drink his blood, ye have no life in you."** (John 6:53) **The onus is on us to pray that we pant for this drink like a deer for God does not force anyone to follow Him. This is a lesson from Jesus that we ought to depend on God day in day out for our spiritual survival not on an individual's opinion.** We are told **"As newborn babes, desire the sincere milk of the word, that ye may grow thereby:" (1 Peter2:2)**

I used to be in huge storm of being a lazy Christian. I found it hard to pray for my own verse and get my own revelation from God. I used to tell myself I was not capable of doing that as I was still young in the Lord. I found myself being young for years on end. If the Pastor or Bible study leader told us to go and read certain chapters, I would wait then find someone to ask what it said. I did not bother memorising verses and when I needed one I would ask the next person. I avoided debates on Biblical ideas because I had nothing to contribute. I gave excuses when asked to share the Word. I was a disgrace.

One of my sons would not crawl until he was 9 months old. I almost consulted a specialist about him. Then one day he woke up crawling, standing and walking at once. I can not describe my elation, relief and joy at this development. Then it occurred to me that if I kept claiming to be young, failing to do what a Christian of so many years should do, probably God felt the same way I felt about my son. I started feeding on first hand Word of God and I literally felt myself crawling, standing and walking at once. Solely depending on others had restrained my growth and I had to practice a personal relationship with God with the help of the church, family and friends.

## *Garbage In Garbage Out*

GIGO, as it is shortened, is an aphorism we learnt when computers first appeared on the scene. It meant invalid input resulted in invalid output. Amazingly it works the same way with the human mind. What you feed it on is what comes out.

Refuse to feed your mind on bad TV and videos, bad computer sites or bad books, impure material, idle and slanderous stuff if you want to soar up like an eagle. That is dead meat, refuse to compromise. What we feed our eyes and ears on is captured in our minds, it is processed into a picture then into words, we then act on the words and these actions can determine our future and destiny. Jesus said:

> **"A good man out of the good treasure of his heart bringeth forth that which is good; and an evil man out of the evil treasure of his heart bringeth forth that which is evil: for of the abundance of the heart his mouth speaketh." ( Luke 6:45 )**

The seed determines the fruit. An apple tree cannot miraculously bear oranges. Select what seed you are going to plant up in your mind. Ask for discernment from the Holy Spirit and you will know what your mind's diet should be. Make this your prayer **"Let the words of my mouth, and the meditation of my heart, be acceptable in thy sight, O LORD, my strength, and my redeemer." (Psalms 19:14)** Not only are we to avoid evil but the Bible says we ought to avoid even what *appears* evil in 1 Thessalonians 5:22. My mother always used to warn us against whispering in the presence of others. No matter how innocent the issue is, the fact that you are whispering, makes it *appear* evil.

Vultures eat anything but eagles eat fresh meat. Stand up for God, pure in what you eat even if that means risking being ridiculed. Act like Daniel who refused to defile himself by eating the king's delicacies. In Daniel 1:8 Daniel resolved not to defile himself with the royal food and wine, and he asked the chief official for permission not to defile himself this way.

> **"Finally, brethren, whatsoever things are true, whatsoever things are honest, whatsoever things are just, whatsoever things are pure, whatsoever things are lovely, whatsoever things are of good report; if there be any virtue, and if there be any praise, think on these things" (Philippians 4:8)**

We have to practice and train our minds to think about such things. We need to guard against impure thoughts as they will determine our speech and actions. A wondering mind is dangerous. It ventures into undesirable territories that are detrimental to the soul. We need to gird up the loins of our minds as 1 Peter 1:13 says. Girding the loins of anything is to secure it and putting it under control. Once we win the battle in the mind we will have put almost everything under control.

I went through rough patches of fearing to do God's work in public. I had a problem in watching the God Channel on TV. I found it unexciting. I was ashamed of reading a gospel book or magazine in public, or playing gospel music in my car or at a party, I feared what people would think about me. When advising someone I avoided giving them Christian advice. I for one was not convinced it worked either. I was selective in discussions, I checked who was around first and manipulated the conversation to suit the audience. I regret the precious time I wasted deceiving no one but myself. I would like to thank God today for His mercy and grace. He clearly showed me that the life I was living was my own and no one else's and if I wasted any minute, I would never gain it back. He reminded me that one day I would be answerable to my actions.

If I was ashamed of Him in that way there was no question of Him intervening in any of my matters. Our Lord Jesus Christ in Luke 9:26 exhorts us that whoever is ashamed of Him, He will also be ashamed of them. He taught me the principle of reciprocity. Whatever I sowed was exactly what I reaped. I learned to think about good things if I wanted a good spiritual shape. I had to make up my mind on whether I wanted to be someone I imagined or to be the person God wanted me to be. I did not have to live an artificial life of suiting situations. Believe me a life of pretence is strenuous, tedious and energy draining because you always have to make serious calculations of where you are and with who. I am now free, the truth set me free. Any action I take now is taken freely without having to enter into the cumbersome drill of wondering what anyone will think. God is the only one who matters.

Spiritual storms are fierce. I conquered one of admitting that my soul could also get hungry and it needed feeding. That admission took years to come by. All along I was busy trying to change what the Word of God declares "wonderfully and fearfully made" in Psalm 139:14. I used to pay a lot of attention to my physical diet only and forgot my spiritual one. God wants us to pay attention to both. The physical body is equally important to look after because it is the temple of God.

> **"Know ye not that ye are the temple of God, and that the Spirit of God dwelleth in you? If any man defile the temple of God, him shall God destroy; for the temple of God is holy, which temple ye are"** (1 Corinthians 3:16-17)

We ought not to mess it. I became ashamed of it when I recognised the consequences of feeding the body and my soul with junk. I made them junk. The Word of God redeemed me and now my aim is to choose a healthy diet for both my body and my spirit, the one described in **Colossians 3:16 – "Let the word of Christ dwell in you richly in all wisdom;….."** Letting the Word dwell in me richly leaves no room for anything impure. I thank God who has helped me to reverse my stance, I now freely sow gospel in my mind, watch it, play it, read it and that way, I reap a healthy gospel filled spirit. May the Lord help you choose your spiritual diet wisely to give you the strength to mount up like an eagle.

# DAILY WORD OF POWER

Ye have seen what I did unto the Egyptians, and how I bare you on eagles' wings, and brought you unto myself. Now therefore, if ye will obey my voice indeed, and keep my covenant, then ye shall be a peculiar treasure unto me above all people: for all the earth is mine:

Exodus 19:4-5

For our light affliction, which is but for a moment, worketh for us a far more exceeding and eternal weight of glory;

2 Corinthians 4:17

Who redeemeth thy life from destruction; who crowneth thee with lovingkindness and tender mercies; Who satisfieth thy mouth with good things; so that thy youth is renewed like the eagle's.

Psal 103:4-5

Notes:

# Chapter 9 RUN NOT GROWING WEARY, WALK NEVER FAINTING

*Perseverance is that last lap you take when you are dead beat*

Our final promise that Isaiah says God gives us when we wait upon Him is running and walking without being weary. When we run we naturally become weary. Maybe we are running and walking while carrying our heavy burdens of problems. Or we are passing through hard times that we can not change in our own power. Maybe we are going down a dark valley of the shadow of death. But like every shadow, the oppressions, difficulties and trials we are facing always look twice their actual size. This makes us so drained that what we need is God's grace. But while this happens, God promises to renew our strength. He will substitute our natural weakness with His supernatural power.

Fainting, results in loss of power, it leads to collapsing and becoming weary. I experienced fainting physically and spiritually. I lost strength many times and had to go back to the Lord to regain it. Fainting even in the natural world is a condition which leaves us in a short lapse of consciousness. Usually when we come to, we need some time to get orientated again. I remember one time I had an operation. The anaesthetic must have played up and when I woke up, I had lost my memory. It is not a pleasant condition at all. I had to pray a lot to regain my memory and strength. With prayer and some memory exercises it was slowly restored. We are minded not to faint but to press on in the hope of triumph through Jesus Christ.

God will certainly renew the strength of those who wait upon Him. We fly, run and walk. In all three activities we are depending on God to lift us and supply the strength we need to endure the stress. If I am totally going to depend on anyone for provision, I would need to know them. I have known of contracts that were signed because a powerful person has phoned to support it or to give guarantee, although the contractors might not have seen them, they oblige because of what they know about that person.

I was self employed registered to do some work for a Government Ministry on demand. All went well for 3 years and some human error caused my services to cease. I knew I had not done anything wrong and I made enquiries. Unfortunately it is an extremely busy department and not every enquiry can be attended to.

Typically I did not get a response and it affected me left right and centre. Eventually God led me to one of the Executives who I believe listened to the Holy Spirit to allow me to see him. He did not ask the Ministry to do anything apart from replying to my inquiry. I immediately received responses and a remedy to the situation. If earthly mighty men can turn the tables around, what about God whose name is I AM? Did He not invite us in Jeremiah 33:3 to call unto Him and He would answer us?

I classed the ordeal into three stages, soaring, running and walking. During the time I was waiting for the answer from work, my financial and social life was muddled. My husband was very supportive and remained optimistic about it. He assisted me in asking God to help me fly like an eagle in this trying time. I had to soar up and glide to a place of safety to remain sane. Then when the case was in the Executive's hands I no longer needed to glide and soar, I began to run. I was still concerned but the pressure was less. I kept on praying fervently and thanking God for taking care of the matter but I had taken a slower exercise of running. When I got the first response I started walking. I was almost at the end of the tunnel and I could see more light. I still walked in prayer and fasting but my speed had reduced to walking steadily.

All the stages were equally important to me and what I appreciated in all of them was that my strength came from God. I have had such cycles in my life, I can fly for months then get weeks of running and days of walking.

I do not get weary because my God supplies me with renewed strength. I wait upon Him for guidance. The situation determines the speed and God takes over as long as we have fully surrendered otherwise if, in the eyes of God we still depend on something else, He lays off. The road is not always smooth and straight but the bigger the problem the bigger the testimony.

The crux of our promises is in this final declaration that they that wait upon the Lord, shall run and not grow weary, they shall walk and never faint. Our God is all sufficient. This is a promise of permanent sustenance, perpetual renewal, everlasting providence and ceaseless assistance. The Bible says there is a season for everything. Everything comes to an end one day. But here we are assured of a never-ending supply of vitality. Is it not overwhelming to comprehend such a concept? But that is how immense and glorious our God is. With Him nothing is impossible. Given that, take a few moments then and weigh the significance of waiting upon the Lord and see if it is not worth reckoning.

## *Fear Not*

Do you believe God can do what He says in this final promise of running and walking? Fear can deter us from believing our promises. Know the Lord and cast out fear because fear begets unbelief. We need to know who we are waiting upon and what He can do. Knowing God was one of the things I paradoxically feared in my Christian walk and that lack of knowledge was one of my roughest patches. I read and reread the Book of Job who was righteous but disaster was allowed to strike. I feared that if I became anything close to what Job was like, I would be prescribing catastrophes. That is the problem of lack of knowledge. The Bible is full of promises that I should not fear, that God is always with me, that I was not given a Spirit of fear!

Knowing Him and incessantly reading and listening to His Word was the ultimatum. I needed Christian books and articles. I needed to communicate with Him in prayer, talking and listening to Him, and to humble myself in fasting. The Lord taught me that in prayer we focus on Him and in fasting He focuses on us. Without a closer walk with God, we will not know Him and we can not trust Him if we do not know Him. We will live in fear resulting in becoming weary and fainting.

When I was expecting my first child I was very anxious about everything. I was surrounded by many well wishers who unintentionally told me conflicting information. I wanted to be sure my child was well fed, was growing and that I was not doing anything to interfere with his development. The Doctor put my mind to rest by advising me to get as much information as I could from medical books and magazines about pregnancy and birth. The more I read the more relaxed I became. The knowledge I gained took away my fear. I learnt what was normal and what was not. I used to be alarmed by certain pains and movements. I discovered from my reading that if those pains and movements did not occur then I should be alarmed.

Through the tuition, I became an expert on pregnancy. I could even advise others to get informed. Jesus said, **"If ye continue in my word, then are ye my disciples indeed; And ye shall know the truth, and the truth shall make you free." (John 8:31-32)** Why do we find fear gnawing inside us for worthless reasons? We fear the unknown and even end up taking the wrong steps. Only the Word reveals the truth about the mighty power of God, His protection and deliverance. Without it we will be incapacitated from flying, running and walking with renewed strength.

The devil uses fear to deceive us and tempt us. If we are consistent in the Word we learn that God said "Fear not", that the devil, although he is real, he is a defeated angel, that he roars like a lion to instil fear in us but he is not a lion. satan knows that fear is a weapon powerful enough to deter and paralyse believers from faith. Fear leads to worry and no one can function in worry.

The good news is that when we know the Word, we know our Father and we can fight the spiritual war in full confidence that He will fight it for us. We can deal with the situation proclaiming the Word. The Word, as already discussed, is the only weapon the devil fears. He tempted Jesus and Jesus told him "it is written...... it is written" and he fled. Get acquainted with God's promises and live in joy and peace. **"For God hath not given us the spirit of fear; but of power, and of love, and of a sound mind." (2 Tim. 1:7)**

Fear is the opposite of faith. Fear not, God is with you. Nothing can separate you from the love of God. Not even the storm you are facing right now. Do not faint. Have faith that God's love will see you safely through it. Whether you are flying, running or walking, remember **"There is no fear in love; but perfect love casteth out fear: because fear hath torment. He that feareth is not made perfect in love." (1 John 4:18)** You are a new creation. Do not dwell on the fear of the past. God takes care of tomorrow do not live in fear of the future. God is our healer, do not live in fear about your health. He is our rock do not live in fear of failure. This earth and its fullness is His, leave your finances in His control. His name is I AM, He is your Ministry, your family, your relations, your friends, your job. Trust Him wherever you want your need met. He has no beginning or end, He is everlasting and eternal. That is why you should fear not, He is with you, do not faint.

What is your fear today? Do not let it destroy you. Have faith. Do not allow it to make you weary. Pray that God takes it away through the power of the Holy Spirit and replace it with faith, love, joy and peace. Fear is only false evidence appearing real.

# DAILY WORD OF VICTORY

**Seek the LORD, and his strength: seek his face evermore.**

**Psalm 105:4**

**And let us not be weary in well doing: for in due season we shall reap, if we faint not.**

**Galatians 6:9**

**I can do all things through Christ which strengtheneth me.**

**Philippians 4:13**

# Chapter 10
# STAND FIRM AND LIVE IN VICTORY

***What is more important prayer or Bible reading? Whatever is more important to the eagle, its right wing or left?***

You remember in chapter 8 I indicated how important it is to have a strong foundation? I would like to recall your attention to it and merge it with a similar function of roots to a tree. What are roots for? Roots are the foundation of the tree. They anchor the tree to the ground, draw water and food for the tree and they sustain the whole tree. It follows then that, weak and shallow roots are incapable of giving their tree stability and food. When winds come they are easily uprooted, when drought comes they wither because the roots are not deep enough. Trees with deeper and thicker roots guarantee life to the whole tree by storing food. Even when you cut such a tree, the stump will produce shoots to revive the tree. The conundrum therefore is this, how deep are your root? Let us examine our walk with God and the storms you have so far encountered will reveal what sort of roots you have in God by the solutions you sought. Paul says we are rooted in Christ – **"As ye have therefore received Christ Jesus the Lord, so walk ye in him: Rooted and built up in him, and stablished in the faith, as ye have been taught, abounding therein with thanksgiving." (Colossians 2:6-7)**

My earlier days in Christ exposed weak and shallow roots. I succumbed to the slightest breeze that blew. I would consult everyone apart from God. I displayed a green leafy life in the eyes of man but I remained unfruitful like the fig tree in Mark 11:12-14. When fig trees are green and leafy they are expected to bear fruits but this particular one had a wrong signal and Jesus cursed it.

Following in the footsteps of Jesus is all or nothing. There is no middle of the road. Only those who are determined to stay on the narrow way and enter through the strait gate will see the Kingdom of God. Only those who stand firm in trusting God will have everlasting life. Here is a final reiteration of one of the many promises: there is perpetuity of God's providence if we remain solidly rooted in Him:

> **"Blessed is the man that trusteth in the LORD, and whose hope the LORD is. For he shall be as a tree planted by the waters, and that spreadeth out her roots by the river, and shall not see when heat cometh, but her**

> **leaf shall be green; and shall not be careful in the year of drought, neither shall cease from yielding fruit." (Jeremiah 17:7-8).**

Take a look again at the parable of the sower in Mark 4 and visualise the importance of being rooted in the Word to be able to stand firm. Most importantly, note that the roots will not eliminate winds and storms, but they will sustain you to remain anchored for you to survive.

Simply putting your trust in the Lord will open the flood gates of a permanent flow of thirst quenching and life giving water. It is not a question of only believing in God but of completely shifting your trust from all else to God. What do you trust in today, your job, bank account, yourself, friends or family? I used to think trusting in riches was out of question for me because I was not rich. Then it occurred to me that as poor as I was I used to spend most of my time thinking about how I could get money and what I would do with it. Automatically I was in the category of those whose security is based on finances not on trusting God.

Then the Lord showed me that trusting in man is fatal. Man will let you down, he will pull you away from the source of strength and you will wither. Stand firm in the Lord and extend your roots in the Word. As your roots grow deeper in the Word while living in this world so fraught with pain, you will not be shaken, you will stand firm. In the year of drought, that is, when calamity strikes, your deep roots will supply you with the living water. You will stand secure when storms rage. God understands all your struggles and pain and He is the only source of life.

Are you content with mediocrity? Do you not mind a season of unfruitfulness? If so you are underestimating the power of the God you believe in, the God of Abraham, Isaac and Jacob, who can ceaselessly supply fruit in all the areas of your life. Fulfil your vision and dream right now. Pray until something happens. Persist like the importunate widow who persisted to get justice in Luke 18. Insist like Abraham who pleaded for the righteous to be saved in Sodom and Gomorrah until the number went down to ten in Genesis 18:20-33. Pray the prayer which my other friend Mrs Fungai Chiwashira calls the birthing prayer. She says at that time when you are agonising in prayer, you are in labour, hang in there and be careful not to kill what you were about to deliver by giving up in the struggle. Stay close to the source of strength by rooting yourself in the Word and in prayer. The heat of disaster shall not be debilitating when your hope is firmly placed in God's hands.

When the Israelites were leaving Egypt, they thanked God that they had left all their problems behind. When they looked back they were dismayed to find their captors following them. In this journey, we know God is with us and directing us. We will see storms coming interfering in our lives. We look back and see the chains of bondage we were released from threatening to bind us again. We will take Moses's stance:

> **"And Moses said unto the people, Fear ye not, stand still, and see the salvation of the Lord, which he will shew to you to day: for the Egyptians whom ye have seen to day, ye shall see them again no more for ever. The Lord shall fight for you, and ye shall hold your peace. (Exodus 14:13-14)**

He told them to stand still and after standing still, they would see the salvation of God. He takes care to mention that they should stand still. As we discussed being still is not becoming motionless, it means paralyse your own efforts and follow God's instructions. I had strained to be still, and sometimes I still do. My mistake was that before I consulted God, I would have called all my friends in panic. As a result I missed God's voice and miracles of deliverance because of other challenges that clamoured my hearing.

Moses told the Israelites that they would not see again the Egyptians they saw. The Red Sea was right in front of them. Behind them the Egyptians were in hot pursuit. Have you ever felt that way? When things go bad you look where you are coming from you see pain and look where you are going and you see horror. God says wait and see. Moses struck the sea and they walked on dry land. We need to exercise our faith and move on. We ask the Holy Spirit to pave dry land in the sea of calamities. We walk on dry land even though on either side the sea monsters are hungrily threatening us.

They crossed the sea and it was true, they did not see the Egyptians again because they drowned. By faith, God's grace will drown all our obstacles. God's desire is to deliver the righteous from the problems they see now. He desires to see us free and free indeed. Even if it seems as if God is delaying, it is not denial. We need to stand still and hear Him then we move on and defeat our current challenges. We wait on Him to give us the go ahead and the strength to accept those things we can not change on our own. We then persevere in His will.

### *Be bold in the Lord*

Faithfulness, boldness and obedience will allow us to stand firm in the Lord and He will deliver us. Let us look at that kind of boldness demonstrated by Esther. Esther was a Jewish orphan who had no idea that one day she would become a Queen. She was raised by her cousin Mordecai and got married to the King of Persia and Media. In those days if any of the King's wives went to see him without being summoned they would be killed. Mordecai told Esther that there was a plot to kill the Jews and asked Esther to persuade the King to save them. Esther and her household fasted for three days about it before approaching the King. Confronting the King was daunting but she was bold and selfless.

> **"Go, gather together all the Jews that are present in Shushan, and fast ye for me, and neither eat nor drink three days, night or day: I also and my maidens will fast likewise; and so will I go in unto the king, which is not**

**according to the law: and if I perish, I perish." (Esther 4:16)**

This was a great risk, but faith is bold and it takes risks knowing fully that God is mighty and able to lift us up. Esther knew it could bode ill on her but she declared that if she perished she perished. She made a bold declaration which meant either way she trusted all would work together for good for her. She knew fasting would bring hope in a hopeless situation. She should not faint in the rough and dark valley but fast. Our heavy burdens become lighter when we know where to anchor to attain victory.

ALL the preceding verses cap it all: trusting in the Lord in whichever season, will bring far-reaching and interminable blessings of victory. Come what may, I urge you to keep your hope and trust immovably anchored in God's true and unfailing promises and the "son-light" will not stop streaming in.

## *Conclusion*

I will leave you with what my mentor gave me years ago and told me to personalise while kneeling down and it read like this, **Psalms 91** (paraphrased by author):

Because I dwell in the shelter of the Most High, I will rest in the shadow of the Almighty. I will say of the LORD, "He is my refuge and my fortress, my God, in whom I trust." Surely He will save me from the fowler's snare and from the deadly pestilence. He will cover me with His feathers, and under His wings I will find refuge; His faithfulness will be my shield and rampart. I will not fear the terror of night, nor the arrow that flies by day, nor the pestilence that stalks in the darkness, nor the plague that destroys at midday. A thousand may fall at my side, ten thousand at my right hand, but it will not come near me. I will only observe with my eyes and see the punishment of the wicked. Because I make the Most High my dwelling— even the LORD, who is my refuge-then no harm will befall me, no disaster will come near my tent. For He will command his angels concerning me to guard me in all my ways; they will lift me up in their hands, so that I will not strike my foot against a stone. I will tread upon the lion and the cobra; I will trample the great lion and the serpent."Because he loves me," says the LORD, "I will rescue him; I will protect him, for he acknowledges my name. He will call upon me, and I will answer him; I will be with him in trouble, I will deliver him and honour him. With long life will I satisfy him and show him my salvation. May you make this your prayer too.

May the Almighty God bless you that you may find courage in your current situation. Proclaim victory now in health, in your work, your finances, for prosperity, His favour, your family and friends, in the Name of Jesus Christ. May His grace rest upon you and may your faith increase from one level to another. Weapons will be formed but no weapon formed against you shall prosper. I pray that the glory of the Lord may manifest in your life, in an amazing way, by the power of the Holy Spirit, through our Lord Jesus Christ. May He destroy all the strongholds, infirmities and barriers of the devil in your life in a way that no eye has seen nor any ear has heard. I pray for a revelation in your endeavours. May He open your spiritual eyes and ears for discernment to give you a deeper understanding for the purpose and meaning of your life. May He give you peace now and the strength to pull through whatever you are undergoing right now. May He open new doors that no one will close, may He make a way in whatever appears like a wilderness. I pray that He gives you all the desires of your heart in His will. Victory is yours, protection is yours, success is yours, blessings are yours, health is yours, in the matchless name of our Lord Jesus Christ, who died and rose again. Amen

**Bibliography**

1. The New Jerome Biblical Commentary: Geoffrey Chapman 1990: Prentice Hall, inc.
2. Good Morning Holy Spirit: Benny Hinn 1990: Thomas Nelson Publishers

All scripture quotations are taken from the *King James Version* of the Bible

Contact Author:

P.O. Box 516
Bury
Lancashire
BL8 9FG
UK

*Email:* claramoyo@yahoo.com

Website: www.claramoyo.wordpress.com

Printed in the United Kingdom
by Lightning Source UK Ltd.
125242UK00002B/76-900/A

9 781434 332936